CONTENTS

D0550851

Unit 6 Recording Cost Information *62*

Standards of Competence

Element 6.1   Operate and maintain a system of accounting for material costs *62*
Element 6.2   Operate and maintain a system of accounting for labour costs *63*
Element 6.3   Operate and maintain a system of accounting for expenses *63*
Element 6.4   Operate and maintain a system for the apportionment and absorption of indirect costs (overheads) *64*

Simulations and Tasks (Elements and performance criteria are shown in brackets)

Unit 8 Preparing VAT Returns   *101*

Standard of Competence
Element 8.1   Prepare VAT Returns   *101*

Simulations and Tasks (Elements and performance criteria are shown in brackets)

PART 3 SUGGESTED ANSWERS   *117*

Simulations

This workbook follows a similar format to that used in the workbook for Accounting at NVQ Level 2, with which you may be familiar. The objectives are similar. Firstly to accompany the textbook, Business Accounting 1, by Frank Wood, and to provide students with business related simulations and tasks with which to apply their knowledge and understanding of accounts. Secondly, to enable candidates to use the simulations and tasks to show some evidence of competence in the accounting programme of the Lead Body for Accounting at NVQ Level 3.

The Units of Competence against which the workbook will help to provide evidence are:

Level 3

Unit Number	Unit Title
4	Recording capital transactions
5	Preparing financial accounts
6	Recording cost information
8	Preparing VAT returns

Evidence can be collected from four main sources:
- prior achievement;
- performance in the workplace;
- performance in the specially set activities;
- questioning: oral, written, or by computer.

The workbook is specifically aimed at the latter two sources.

The Qualification Structure of the AAT to enable students to satisfy the requirements at NVQ Level 3 is as follows:

Level 3

Unit Number	Unit Title
4	Recording capital transactions
5	Preparing financial accounts
6	Recording cost information
7	Preparing reports and returns
8	Preparing VAT returns
21	Information technology environment
22	Using spreadsheets
25	Health and safety

Candidates will need to refer to *Business Accounting 1* (see cross references to relevant chapters at the foot of each page) and will require tutorial support before undertaking the simulations and tasks in the workbook. Included in the workbook are Step-by-Step Guides to assist the candidate in Unit 5 – Preparing Financial Accounts. It may be necessary to refer to costing textbooks e.g. *Managerial Accounting and Finance*, by Frank Wood and Joe Townsley (Pitman Publishing) to assist in the study of Unit 6 – Recording Cost Information.

Accompanying all simulations is full documentation to enable the tasks to be carried out by the candidate.

Each section is a separate Unit and starts with an extract from the Standards of Competence. This includes the Unit Title, constituent Elements and the Performance Criteria applicable to each element. The Performance Criteria define what constitutes competent performance. The Range Statement defines the situations, contexts, methods, etc, in which the competence should be displayed. The Knowledge and Understanding required for each Element is defined under subsections i.e. Accounting Techniques, Accounting Principle Theory and The Organisation. See the following example:

Performance Criteria

Unit 4   Recording Capital Transactions

Element 4.1 Maintain records and accounts relating to capital expenditure

a   Relevant details relating to specific items of capital expenditure are correctly entered in the appropriate records

b   The organisation's records agree with the physical presence of capital items

c   Any acquisition and disposal costs and revenues are correctly identified and recorded

d   Depreciation charges and other necessary entries and adjustments are correctly calculated and recorded in the appropriate ledger accounts

e   Where required, the records show clearly the prior authority for capital expenditure and indicate the approved method of funding

f   The organisation's policies, regulations, procedures and timescales are observed

g   Discrepancies, unusual features or queries are identified and either resolved or referred to the appropriate person

Each Performance Criterion has been identified: For example,
    a Relevant details relating to specific ......

This identification is used in both the simulation and tasks and in the Record of Assessment located at the front of the workbook on pages 3–8.

Now turn to the first simulation – 1(A). Successful completion will indicate competence against Performance Criteria 4.1 a, c, f. Completing the other simulations and tasks in this section will indicate additional competence. On the Record of Assessment sheet, the competence shown can be recorded. For example:

Element 4.1 Maintain records and accounts relating to capital expenditure

Performance Criteria	Evidence of Competence	Date	Checked
c Any acquisition and disposal costs and revenues are correctly identified and recorded	*Simulation 1A (Tasks 1, 2 and 3)*	*4.3.94*	*AG*

As the portfolio of evidence is accumulated it will be possible to refer to the workbook as support for evidence of competence. The same format is used for subsequent units.

Where the title of the simulation is followed by ^A the answer will be found at the back of the book. Those simulations and tasks without the ^A suffix have their answers in a separate book, available to lecturers free who recommend Frank Wood's Workbook on their courses.

This workbook has been designed to assist the student by providing simulations and tasks together with all the documentation material required for their completion. This will enable students to work in class or independently and to check their work using the fully worked answers.

All the situations have been written to reflect realistic business situations but all individuals and firms which appear in them are imaginary. Any reference to a specific individual or firm is purely coincidental.

ACKNOWLEDGEMENTS

I would like to take this opportunity to thank my friends and colleagues, both past and present, of the Management and Business Studies Department at Stockport College of Further and Higher Education for their suggestions, ideas and contributions.

My thanks to Pat Jepson and Sheila Thorn for their valuable assistance. I am particularly grateful to Frank Wood for his support and guidance and finally wish to express my thanks to my family for their contributions, support and encouragement.

The VAT 100 form in Unit 8 is reproduced with the permission of the Controller of Her Majesty's Stationery Office.

I would like to thank the following organisations who gave me permission to use their past examination questions and documentation to assist candidates in undertaking the tasks.

The Association of Accounting Technicians
The Chartered Institute of Bankers
The Chartered Institute of Marketing
H.M. Inland Revenue
H.M. Customs and Excise
Lead Body for Accounting

Sheila I. Robinson
1993

Part 1

RECORD OF ASSESSMENT

Record of Assessment

Candidate's Name

UNIT 4   RECORDING CAPITAL TRANSACTIONS

Element 4.1   Maintain records and accounts relating to capital expenditure

Performance Criteria	Evidence of Competence	Date	Checked
a Relevant details relating to specific items of capital expenditure are correctly entered in the appropriate records			
b The organisation's records agree with the physical presence of capital items			
c Any acquisition and disposal costs and revenues are correctly identified and recorded			
d Depreciation charges and other necessary entries and adjustments are correctly calculated and recorded in the appropriate ledger accounts			
e Where required, the records show clearly the prior authority for capital expenditure and indicate the approved method of funding			
f The organisation's policies, regulations, procedures and timescales are observed			
g Discrepancies, unusual features or queries are identified and either resolved or referred to the appropriate person			

Assessed by _____   Date _____   Verified by _____   Date _____

Record of Assessment

Candidate's Name

UNIT 5   PREPARING FINANCIAL ACCOUNTS

Element 5.1   Record income and expenditure

Performance Criteria	Evidence of Competence	Date	Checked
a Income and expenditure is correctly recorded in the appropriate ledger accounts			
b Any accrued or prepaid income and expenditure is correctly identified and adjustments made			
c The organisation's policies, regulations, procedures and timescales are observed			
d Income and expenditure is analysed in accordance with defined requirements and appropriate information is passed to management			
e Discrepancies, unusual features or queries are identified and either resolved or referred to the appropriate person			

Assessed by _____   Date _____   Verified by _____   Date _____

Element 5.2   Prepare accounts from incomplete records

Performance Criteria	Evidence of Competence	Date	Checked
a Essential accounts and reconciliations are correctly prepared			
b Existing primary information is accurately summarised			
c Other relevant information is correctly identified and recorded			
d Investigations into the client's business transactions are conducted with tact and courtesy			
e The organisation's policies, regulations, procedures and timescales are observed			
f Discrepancies, unusual features or queries are identified and either resolved or referred to the appropriate person			

Assessed by _____   Date _____   Verified by _____   Date _____

Element 5.3   Prepare the extended trial balance

Performance Criteria	Evidence of Competence	Date	Checked
a The trial balance is accurately extended and totalled			
b Totals from the general ledger or other records are correctly entered on the extended trial balance			
c Any errors disclosed by the trial balance are traced and corrected			
d Any adjustments not dealt with in the ledger accounts are correctly entered on the extended trial balance			
e An agreed valuation of closing stock is correctly entered on the extended trial balance			
f The organisation's policies, regulations, procedures and timescales are observed			
g Discrepancies, unusual features or queries are identified and either resolved or referred to the appropriate person			

Assessed by _____   Date _____   Verified by _____   Date _____

Record of Assessment

Candidate's Name

UNIT 6   RECORDING COST INFORMATION

Element 6.1   Operate and maintain a system of accounting for material costs

Performance Criteria	Evidence of Competence	Date	Checked
a Data are correctly coded, analysed and recorded			
b Standard costs for materials are established in accordance with the organisation's procedures			
c Materials issued from stores are correctly priced in accordance with the organisation's policy			
d Materials issued are systematically checked against the organisation's overall usage and stock control practices and unusual issues reported to management			
e Timely information on materials usage is accurately presented to management			
f Any queries are either resolved immediately or referred to the appropriate person			

Assessed by _____   Date _____   Verified by _____   Date _____

Element 6.2   Operate and maintain a system of accounting for labour costs

Performance Criteria	Evidence of Competence	Date	Checked
a Data are correctly coded, analysed and recorded			
b Standard labour costs are established in accordance with the organisation's procedures			
c Labour costs are calculated in accordance with the organisation's policies and procedures			
d Timely information relating to labour utilisation is presented accurately to management			
e Staff working in operational departments are consulted to resolve any queries in the data			

Assessed by _____   Date _____   Verified by _____   Date _____

Element 6.3 Operate and maintain a system of accounting for expenses

Performance Criteria	Evidence of Competence	Date	Checked
a Data are correctly coded, analysed and recorded			
b Standard costs for expenses are established in accordance with the organisation's procedures			
c Information relating to expenses is accurately and clearly presented to management			
d Staff working in operational departments are consulted to resolve any queries in the data			

Assessed by _____ Date _____ Verified by _____ Date _____

Element 6.4 Operate and maintain a system for the apportionment and absorption of indirect costs (overheads)

Performance Criteria	Evidence of Competence	Date	Checked
a Overhead costs are correctly attributed to direct cost centres and cost units in accordance with agreed methods of apportionment and absorption			
b Adjustments for under/over recorded overheads are made in accordance with established procedures			
c Methods of overhead apportionment and absorption are reviewed at regular intervals in discussion with senior staff			
d Staff working in operational departments are consulted to resolve any queries in the data			

Assessed by _____ Date _____ Verified by _____ Date _____

7

Record of Assessment

Candidate's Name

UNIT 8   PREPARING VAT RETURNS

Element 8.1   Prepare VAT returns

Performance Criteria	Evidence of Competence	Date	Checked
a VAT returns are correctly completed from the appropriate sources and submitted within the statutory time limits			
b Relevant inputs and outputs are correctly identified and calculated			
c VAT documentation is correctly filed			
d Submissions are made in accordance with currently operative VAT laws and regulations			
e Discussions with VAT inspectors are conducted openly and constructively to promote the efficiency of the VAT accounting system			

Assessed by _____   Date _____   Verified by _____   Date _____

Part 2

STANDARDS OF COMPETENCE

FOR ACCOUNTING AT NVQ LEVEL 3

Recording Capital Transactions

Standards of Competence

ELEMENT 4.1 MAINTAIN RECORDS AND ACCOUNTS RELATING TO CAPITAL EXPENDITURE

Performance Criteria

a Relevant details relating to specific items of capital expenditure are correctly entered in the appropriate records

b The organisation's records agree with the physical presence of capital items

c Any acquisition and disposal costs and revenues are correctly identified and recorded

d Depreciation charges and other necessary entries and adjustments are correctly calculated and recorded in the appropriate ledger accounts

e Where required, the records show clearly the prior authority for capital expenditure and indicate the approved method of funding

f The organisation's policies, regulations, procedures and timescales are observed

g Discrepancies, unusual features or queries are identified and either resolved or referred to the appropriate person

Range Statement

- Entries relating to tax allowances are excluded
- Depreciation methods: straight line, reducing balance
- Discrepancies, unusual features or queries include lack of agreement between physical items and records

Knowledge and Understanding

This Unit assumes competence in Units 1 and 2.

The business environment
- Types and characteristics of different types of asset
- Main requirements of SSAP 12 or any relevant FRS
- Relevant legislation and regulations (public sector organisations)

Accounting techniques
- Methods of depreciation
- Accounting treatment of capital items sold, scrapped or otherwise retired from service
- Use of plant registers and similar subsidiary records
- Use of transfer journal

Accounting principles and theory

- Basic accounting concepts and principles – matching of income and expenditure within an accounting period, historic cost, accruals, consistency, prudence, materiality
- Principles of double entry accounting
- Distinction between capital and revenue expenditure, what constitutes capital expenditure

The organisation

Background understanding that the accounting systems of an organisation are affected by its organisational structure, its administrative systems and procedures and the nature of its business transactions

Capital and Revenue Expenditure Exercises

Unit 4
Recording Capital Transactions
Element 4.1
Maintain records and accounts relating to capital expenditure Performance criteria **a c f**

▶**Task 1**

Indicate which of the following would be revenue items and which would be capital items in a clothing manufacturing business:

(a) Purchase of new sewing machine
(b) Repairs to sewing machine
(c) Purchase of six pairs of cutting scissors
(d) Decorating the canteen
(e) Electricity account for both office and works
(f) New photocopier for office
(g) Installation of security system
(h) Wages of machinists
(i) Material for use in manufacture
(j) New printer for computer

▶**Task 2**

From the following items of expenditure of 'Morgans' Garage' classify them between capital and revenue expenditure:

(a) Stationery
(b) Purchase of breakdown vehicle
(c) Trolley jack
(d) Overalls for workmen
(e) Telephone account
(f) Vehicle lift
(g) Insurance
(h) Lubricating oil pump
(i) Wages of workmen for decorating office
(j) Hand cleaner

▶**Task 3**

For the business of Penhalls Advertising & Marketing Co. identify from the following list those items of capital and revenue expenditure:

(a) Cost of printing business cards for own use
(b) Purchase of new car for Marketing Manager
(c) Entertainment charges incurred on visiting new clients
(d) Heating and lighting – quarterly account
(e) Joiners account for supplying and fitting new shelves in offices
(f) Office files, punch and sundry stationery items
(g) Monthly petrol account
(h) College fees for new trainee
(i) New office safe
(j) Cost of installing office safe

SIMULATION 2

Holly Dale Hotel

Background information

Geoff worked for many years as a commercial banker but at the recent reorganisation of the staff he decided to take early retirement. One of his and his wife's ambitions has been to own and run a small hotel in the Lake District catering for walkers and climbers. Geoff and Anne are both keen walkers and have been members of walking clubs for many years.

Holly Dale Hotel is situated near Grasmere in its own grounds of approximately one and a half acres. All its six bedrooms are en-suite and amongst its facilities are a dining room, lounge and two other rooms which can be used for storing climbing and walking equipment and a drying room.

Structurally the Hotel is sound and the previous owners have kept up with the maintenance and some refurbishment.

Geoff and Anne have now moved into the private flat situated at the rear of the Hotel. They have decided to proceed cautiously with the upgrading of certain parts of the Hotel and have produced a budget for the first year's expenditure.

▶Task 1

From the attached list classify the following items as either Capital or Revenue Expenditure prior to the books, papers, etc being forwarded to Geoff and Anne's accountant.

HOLLY DALE HOTEL GRASMERE

Items of Expenditure

One double and two single beds
10 feather pillows (purchased as a special offer
 @ £5.00 each including a free pillow case)
Bathroom suites
Labour to plumb in bathroom suites
Curtains
Carpeting
Table linen
Cutlery
Vase and dried flower arrangement
Reception desk
Stationery
Portable typewriter
6 waste-paper bins
Towels
Toilet rolls and tissues
Soap and bubble bath
Road tax on estate car
Garage repair account re: estate car
Estate car (second-hand)

BA1 Ch 20, 24

2 boxes pansies and wallflowers
6 rose bushes
2 five-litre tins emulsion paint ⎫ Geoff is going to do
20 rolls of wallpaper and paste ⎬ his own decorating
2 storage heaters for drying room ⎭
Coat and shoe racks for drying room
   (local joiner to provide materials and labour for making and fitting)

▶Task 2

Although Geoff has years of banking experience he is not too familiar with some of the terms used by the accountancy profession. He drops you a line requesting the following explanations:

(a) Could you please explain to me the difference between 'Capital' and 'Revenue Expenditure' and why it is so important to make the distinction before I enter the invoices into the books of account.

(b) You also mentioned I could depreciate some items like the estate car, furniture and fittings etc. Whilst I understand that depreciation refers to the loss in value of an item, I'm not sure how this affects us in our business capacity. Could you please explain its relevance? Is there more than one method of providing for depreciation? Our neighbouring farmer was telling me he used the Revaluation Method for his livestock.

Draft a suitable reply to Geoff.

SIMULATION 3^A

Laser Printer Depreciation

Background information

On 1 January 19X1 a business purchased a laser printer costing £1,800. The printer has an estimated life of 4 years after which it will have no residual value.

It is expected that the output from the printer will be:

Year	Sheets Printed
19X1	35,000
19X2	45,000
19X3	45,000
19X4	55,000
	180,000

▶ **Task 1**

Calculate the annual depreciation charges for 19X1, 19X2, 19X3 and 19X4 on the laser printer on the following bases:

(i) the straight line basis,
(ii) the diminishing balance method at 60% per annum, and
(iii) the units of output method.

Note: Your workings should be to the nearest £.

▶ **Task 2**

Suppose that in 19X4 the laser printer were to be sold on 1 July for £200 and that the business had chosen to depreciate it at 60% per annum using the diminishing balance method applied on a month for month basis.

Reconstruct the following accounts for 19X4 ONLY:

(i) the Laser Printer account
(ii) the Provision for Depreciation – Laser Printer account, and
(iii) the Assets Disposals account.

Association of Accounting Technicians

SIMULATION 4

Muldane plc

Unit 4
Recording Capital Transactions
Element 4.1
Maintain records and accounts relating to capital expenditure Performance criteria **a c d f g**

Background information

The financial year of Muldane plc ended on 31 May 19X9.

At 1 June 19X8 the company owned motor vehicles costing £124,000 which had been depreciated by a total of £88,000.

On 1 August 19X8 Muldane plc sold motor vehicles which had cost £54,000 and which had been depreciated by £49,000 for £3,900 and purchased new motor vehicles costing £71,000.

It is the policy of Muldane plc to depreciate its motor vehicles at 35% per annum using the diminishing balance method. A full year's depreciation is charged on all motor vehicles in use at the end of each year. No depreciation is charged for the year on assets disposed of during that year.

▶ Task 1

Identify the four factors which can cause fixed assets to depreciate.

▶ Task 2

Which of these four factors is the most important for each of the following fixed assets?

(i) a 90-year lease on a building
(ii) land
(iii) a forest of mature trees to be felled for timber
(iv) a stamping press after the launch of an improved press capable of increased output of higher quality at lower cost.

▶ Task 3

Show the following accounts as they would appear in the ledger of Muldane plc *for the year ended 31 May 19X9 only*:

(i) the Motor Vehicles Account
(ii) The Provision for Depreciation – Motor Vehicles Account, and
(iii) The Assets Disposals Account.

Association of Accounting Technicians

SIMULATION 5

Unit 4
Recording Capital Transactions
Element 4.1
Maintain records and accounts relating to capital expenditure Performance criteria **a c d f g**

John Peacock

Background information

On 1 April 19X8, John Peacock Limited, a recently formed transport company, bought a second-hand lorry at a cost of £40,000. The lorry required immediate repairs costing £5,000 to make it roadworthy; these repairs were completed by 1 May 19X8 when the lorry was brought into service by the company.

Upon acquiring the lorry, John Peacock Limited insured it at an annual premium of £1,200 which was paid immediately.

On 1 July 19X8 the lorry was damaged slightly in a road accident necessitating repairs costing £600; the company decided not to make a claim against the insurance company.

John Peacock Limited has decided to provide for depreciation on the motor lorry on the straight line basis from 1 May 19X8 assuming an expected useful economic life in the business of 5 years and an estimated nil residual value at the end of that period.

▶Task

Prepare the following accounts in the books of John Peacock Limited for the year ended 31 October 19X8:

Motor lorry, at cost, A/c
Motor lorry provision for depreciation A/c
Motor lorry insurance A/c.

Association of Accounting Technicians

Sharp Edge Engineering Co. Ltd

Background information

Since 1 October 19X7, the Sharp Edge Engineering Company Limited has been building up its own customers' delivery service and accordingly has purchased the following vehicles:

19X7
1 October   Van   E676TVX costing £28,000.00
19X8
1 January   Lorry   E438CBA costing £36,000.00
19X9
1 February Van   E779GMS costing £16,000.00
1 July   Van   F934KTA costing £24,000.00

Additional information:

1   Lorry E438CBA proved to be unsuitable for the company's trade and was therefore sold on 31 December 19X8 to John Kerry for £21,680.00.

2   Van E779GMS was bought second-hand. Before joining the company's transport fleet on 1 April 19X9, this van was converted to meet the company's requirements. The conversion work was carried out in the company's own workshops, the following costs being incurred:

	£
Direct labour	1,880.00
Direct materials	3,200.00
Variable overheads	1,370.00

Fixed overheads apportionment added at 25% of prime cost.

3   It is the company's policy to provide depreciation on motor vehicles at the rate of 20% per annum on cost.

4   The company has a contract with the Fairdeal Insurance Company Limited under which each vehicle in the transport fleet is insured at an annual premium of £5,000.00; the first premium for each vehicle is paid the day the vehicle is bought.

5   The company's accounting year end is 30 September.

▶**Task**

Prepare the following accounts where relevant for each of the years ended 30 September 19X8 and 19X9 in the books of the Sharp Edge Engineering Company Limited:

Motor vehicles, at cost, A/c
Motor vehicles provision for depreciation A/c
Lorry E438CBA disposal A/c
Motor vehicles insurance A/c

Association of Accounting Technicians

SIMULATION 7

Unit 4
Recording Capital Transactions
Element 4.1
Maintain records and accounts relating to capital expenditure
Performance criteria **a b c d e f g**

Work-based Assessment on Procedures for Acquisition of Capital Items

You are required to investigate and analyse your own employers' procedures for the acquisition of items of capital expenditure and present your findings in a suitable report form, preferably word-processed.

Include such things as the initial authorisation, which might be part of the company's annual budget. Review the procedure for both the raising of orders and who is responsible for signing them on behalf of the organisation. Does this vary according to different levels of expenditure? Can orders be met by using any supplier or are there specific suppliers with whom the orders must be placed? Investigate the procedure from receipt of invoice to payment authorisation and who is responsible for entering the asset in the company's plant register. What is the procedure for periodically checking the asset's existence? Which method of depreciation is used and are assets depreciated proportionately from date of acquisition or annually irrespective of purchase date?

Preparing Financial Accounts

Elements

5.1 Record income and expenditure
5.2 Prepare accounts from incomplete records
5.3 Prepare the Extended Trial Balance

Standards of Competence

ELEMENT 5.1 RECORD INCOME AND EXPENDITURE

Performance Criteria

a Income and expenditure is correctly recorded in the appropriate ledger accounts

b Any accrued or prepaid income and expenditure is correctly identified and adjustments made

c The organisation's policies, regulations, procedures and timescales are observed

d Income and expenditure is analysed in accordance with defined requirements and appropriate information is passed to management

e Discrepancies, unusual features or queries are identified and either resolved or referred to the appropriate person

Range Statement

• Items of income and expenditure for an organisation, including capital receipts and payments

Knowledge and Understanding

This Unit assumes competence in Units 1, 2 and 3

The business environment
• General function and status of SSAPs and FRSs

Accounting techniques
• Accounting treatment of accruals and prepayments
• Use of transfer journal
• Methods of analysing income and expenditure

Accounting principles and theory
• Principles of double entry accounting
• Basic accounting concepts and principles – matching of income and expenditure within an accounting period, historic cost, accruals, consistency, prudence, materiality
• Function and form of accounts for income and expenditure

The organisation
Background understanding that the accounting systems of an organisation are affected by its organisational structure, its administrative systems and procedures and the nature of its business transactions

ELEMENT 5.2 PREPARE ACCOUNTS FROM INCOMPLETE RECORDS

Performance Criteria

a Essential accounts and reconciliations are correctly prepared

b Existing primary information is accurately summarised

c Other relevant information is correctly identified and recorded

d Investigations into the client's business transactions are conducted with tact and courtesy

e The organisation's policies, regulations, procedures and timescales are observed

f Discrepancies, unusual features or queries are identified and either resolved or referred to the appropriate person

Range Statement

- Reconstructing any accounts from data in an unusual or incomplete form
- Discrepancies, unusual features or queries include situations where insufficient data has been provided, where there are inconsistencies within the data

Knowledge and Understanding

This Unit assumes competence in Units 1, 2, and 3

The business environment
- General function and status of SSAPs and FRSs
- Need to present accounts in the correct form
- Legal, VAT and tax requirements
- Main requirements of SSAPs 2, 5, 9, 12, 13, 21, or any relevant FRSs as they affect this element

Accounting techniques
- Accounting treatment of accruals and prepayments
- Use of transfer journal
- Methods of restructuring accounts from incomplete evidence
- Correction of different types of error
- Making and adjusting provisions

Accounting principles and theory
- Function and form of a trial balance
- Basic principles of stock valuation: cost or NRV; what is included in cost
- Objectives of making provisions for depreciation and other purposes

The organisation
Background understanding that the accounting systems of an organisation are affected by its organisational structure, its administrative systems and procedures and the nature of its business transactions

ELEMENT 5.3 PREPARE THE EXTENDED TRIAL BALANCE

Performance Criteria

a The Trial Balance is accurately extended and totalled

b Totals from the general ledger or other records are correctly entered on the Extended Trial Balance

c Any errors disclosed by the Trial Balance are traced and corrected

d Any adjustments not dealt with in the ledger accounts are correctly entered on the Extended Trial Balance

e An agreed valuation of closing stock is correctly entered on the Extended Trial Balance

f The organisation's policies, regulations, procedures and timescales are observed

g Discrepancies, unusual features or queries are identified and either resolved or referred to the appropriate person

- Relevant accounting policies include the treatment of depreciation and other provisions

This Unit assumes competence in Units 1, 2 and 3

The business environment

- General function and status of SSAPs and FRSs
- Main requirements of SSAPs 2, 5, 9, 12, 13, 21, as they affect this element and any relevant FRSs

Accounting techniques

- Accounting treatment of accruals and prepayments
- Use of transfer journal
- Correction of different types of error
- Making and adjusting provisions

Accounting principles and theory

- Principles of double entry accounting
- Basic accounting concepts and principles – matching of income and expenditure within an accounting period, historic cost, accruals, consistency, prudence, materiality
- Function and form of a Trial Balance
- Basic principles of stock valuation: cost or NRV; what is included in cost
- Objectives of making provisions for depreciation and other purposes

The organisation

Background understanding that the accounting systems of an organisation are affected by its organisational structure, its administrative systems and procedures and the nature of its business transactions

Authors's Note

Re: Unit 5 Preparing Financial Accounts
Element 5.1 Record income and expenditure

Interpretation of the performance criteria is apt to be imprecise. For this reason, the author requests students to refer to *Business Accounting 1*, Chapters 1 – 5 for basic recording of income and expenditure via double entry. Chapter 23 deals with adjustments of income and expenditure (accruals and prepayments) and Chapter 24 distinguishes between capital and revenue expenditure. This topic is covered under Unit 4 Recording Capital Transactions in this workbook.

Income and expenditure is also dealt with via non-profit making organisations, for example clubs, societies, etc. It was felt that it would be beneficial to include some exercises on these types of organisation to give students the opportunity to put theory into practice. Many may wish to claim competences in these areas for their portfolios, particularly if they act as Treasurer for their own club or society.

Step-by-step Guide to Incomplete Records

1   Prepare a Statement of Affairs (i.e. Opening Balance Sheet) of opening items to ascertain:

Initial Capital – (N.B. Include opening Cash/Bank Balance – See Bank A/c).

2   *Either* draw up and balance a Cash + Bank Summary

or If a Cash + Bank Summary is given in the question it may only be necessary to balance it off.

Note Remember Final Cash + Bank Balances to be included in the Final Balance Sheet.

3   Prepare a Working Sheet – it may be necessary to calculate such things as:

(Refer to first exercise in this Unit – Mary Grimes – 15^A)

(a) *Purchases*

	£
Payments – Bank	72,000
Discounts Rec'd	1,100
	73,100
Less Opening creditors	4,700
	68,400
Add Closing creditors	2,590
Purchases	70,990

(b) *Sales*

	£
Received – Bank	96,000
Less Opening debtors	7,320
	88,680
Add Closing debtors	9,500
Sales	98,180

(c) *Accrual – Rent & Rates*

	£
Paid – Bank	2,600
Less In arrear 1/9/X7	200
	2,400
Add In arrear 1/9/X8	260
Rent & Rates	£2,660

(d) *Prepayment – Insurance*

	£
Paid – Bank	800
Add – Prepaid 1/9/X7	160
	960
Less Prepaid 1/9/X8	200
Insurance	£760

4   **Depreciation** – The question may indicate the amount of depreciation to be allowed for or alternatively you may have to compare the value of the asset at the beginning of the period with that at the end of the period – the difference is depreciation.

However, ensure that there have been no additions to assets. If there have been take these into consideration.

5   Prepare the Final Accounts:

Trading A/c
Profits & Loss A/c
Balance Sheet.

Step-by-step Guide to Preparation of Final Accounts

Final Accounts are often prepared from a Trial Balance, and the following guidelines should help to ensure speed and accuracy in their preparation, and ensure that confidence and competence is achieved.

1   Before starting the exercise, rule lines across each item. This avoids picking up a wrong figure – easily done under the stress of an examination.

2   Decide where each item is going *before* you start to prepare the Final Accounts, i.e.

Manufacturing Accounts (*Abbreviation*: Mfr. A/c)
Trading Account (*Abbreviation*: T A/c)
Profit & Loss Account (*Abbreviation*: P & L A/c)
Balance Sheet (*Abbreviation*: B/S).

3   An almost 100% rule!!

- Each item displayed in the Trial Balance must only be entered *once* in the Final Accounts.

- Any item usually at the foot of a Trial Balance exercise should be dealt with *twice*, (i.e. when an item is prepaid at the date of the Final Accounts).

- *Exception to the 100% rule!*
  In the case of Limited companies showing information on their Authorised and Issued Capital:

  Enter Issued Capital *once* in Balance Sheet.
  Enter the Authorised Capital *once* at the foot of the Balance Sheet.

Step-by-step Guide to Deal with Adjustments in Final Accounts

1 **Returns inwards and Returns outwards**

   (i) Returns inwards – deduct from Sales in Trading A/c
   (ii) Returns outwards – deduct from Purchases in Trading A/c

2 **Carriage inwards and Carriage outwards**

   (i) Carriage inwards – add to Purchases in Trading A/c
   (ii) Carriage outwards – charge as an expense in P & L A/c

3 **Prepayments (amounts paid in advance)**

   (i) *Deduct* amount from Expenses in Trial Balance
   (ii) *Add* amount to Debtors in Trial Balance

4 **Accruals (amounts owing)**

   (i) *Add* amount to Expense in Trial Balance
   (ii) *Add* amount to Creditors in Trial Balance

5 **Depreciation**

Straight line or on cost
   (i) Find cost price of asset (say)   £24,000
   (ii) Using percentage given (say)   20%
      calculate 20% of £24,000   =   £4,800
   then

   (a) Charge £4,800 as an expense in P & L A/c
   (b) In B/S deduct *total* depreciation (i.e. £4,800 from this year plus any depreciation deducted in previous years see figure on credit side in Trial Balance) from cost price of asset (£24,000) to arrive at NBV (Net Book Value)

Reducing balance or written down value
   (i) Find cost price of asset (say)   £10,000
   (ii) Find total amount of depreciation
      deducted to date (see credit side
      of Trial Balance) say   £4,000
   (iii) Find the difference   £6,000
   (iv) Using percentage given (say)   10%
      calculate 10% of £6,000   =   £ 600
   then

   (a) Charge £600 as an expense in P & L A/c
   (b) In B/S deduct *total* depreciation (i.e. £600 from this year plus any depreciation deducted in previous years, £4,000, see figure on credit side in Trial Balance) from cost price

6 **Bad Debts Provision**

Creation
(i) Decide on the amount of provision to be created (say 1% of Debtors of £5,000 = £50)

then

(a) Charge the provision £50 to P & L A/c as an expense
(b) In B/S deduct provision £50 from Debtors

Increase in provision
(i) Calculate the new provision (i.e. this year's)
(ii) Find out the old provision (i.e. last year's – look in Trial Balance – credit side)
(iii) Find the difference

then

(a) Charge the *difference* only to P & L A/c
(b) Deduct the *new provision* from Debtors in Balance Sheet

Reduction in provision
(i) Calculate the new provision (i.e. this year's)
(ii) Find out the old provision (i.e. last year's – look in Trial Balance – credit side)
(iii) Find the difference

then

(a) Add back the difference as *income* in P & L A/c
(b) Deduct the *new provision* from Debtors in Balance Sheet

7 **Bad Debts**
Simply write off as an expense in P & L A/c

Model Layout of Final Accounts for Sole Trader

TRADING & PROFIT & LOSS A/C OF . . . . . . FOR THE YEAR ENDED	£	£
Sales		xxx
Less Returns inwards		xx
		xxx
Less Cost of goods sold		
Opening stock	x	
Add Purchases	x	
Add Carriage inwards	x	
Add Wages (occasionally – see Q)	x	
	xx	
Less Returns outwards	x	
	xx	
Less Closing stock	x	xxx
GROSS PROFIT		xxx
Less Expenses		
Bad Debts (written off)	x	
Wages & salaries	x	
Rates	x	
Insurance	x	
Rent	x	
General expenses	x	
Postages	x	
Stationery	x	
Carriage outwards	x	
Discounts allowed	x	
Heating	x	
Electricity	x	
Depreciation	x	
Increase in provision for bad debts	x	xxx
		xxx
Add Income		
Discounts + interest received	x	
Reductions in provision for bad debts	x	xx
NET PROFIT		£xxx

BALANCE SHEET OF . . . . AS AT	COST	TOTAL DEPRECIATION	NET BOOK VALUE
Fixed assets	£	£	£
Premises	X	X	X
Motor vehicle	X	X	X
Office furniture	X	X	X
Office equipment	X	X	X
Machinery	X	X	X
	XX	XX	X
Current assets			
Stock (closing)	X		
Debtors (*Less* Provision for bad debts)	X		
Prepayment	X		
Cash at bank	X		
Cash in hand	X	XX	
Less Current liabilities			
Creditors	X		
Expenses owing	X		
Bank overdraft	X	XX	
NET CURRENT ASSETS			XX
			XXX
Less Long-term liabilities			
Long-term loan			X
			£XXX
Financed by:			
Capital			XXX
Add Profit			X
			XXX
Less Drawings			X
			£XXX

Waterfall Social Club

Background information

On 1st June 19X2 the assets and liabilities of the Waterfall Social Club which meets during the evenings in rented accommodation were as follows:

	£
Stocks of food	150
Cash in hand	820
Creditor for food supplies	72

During the year to 31st May 19X3 the club received and paid the following amounts:

Receipts	£	Payments	£
Subscriptions	3,480	Payments to supplies of food	700
Coffee morning	142	Rent & rates	1,500
Jumble sales	421	Cleaners' wages	1,900
Sale of food, etc.	880	Cleaners' materials	152
Dance proceeds	1,179	Treasurer's expenses	275
		Secretarial expenses	345
		Hi-fi system	1,220

On 31st May 19X3 the club owed £80 for food supplied, but all stocks had been sold.

▶**Task 1**

Calculate the accumulated fund on 1st June 19X2.

▶**Task 2**

Calculate the amount of cash which should be in hand on 31st May 19X3.

▶**Task 3**

Prepare an Income and Expenditure Account for the year ended 31st May 19X3 and a Balance Sheet as at 31st May 19X3.

The Monarchs MMC Club

Background information

The Monarchs MCC is a club for motorcycle enthusiasts.

The club secretary has prepared the following summary of the club's cash and bank transactions for the year ended 31 May 19X9.

The Monarchs MCC
Receipts and Payments Account for the year ended 31 May 19X9

	£		£
Cash and bank balances b/f	540	Secretarial expenses	440
Members' subscriptions	6,127	Rent and rates	2,750
Donations	350	Meeting expenses	2,200
Sales of regalia	1,880	Annual affiliation fee to	
		National Body	500
		Purchases of regalia	1,145
		Purchases of garage tools	583
		Stationery and printing	345
		Cash and bank balances c/f	934
	8,897		8,897

On 1 June 19X8 the club owned garage tools which had cost £2,115 and which were valued at £1,550. Garage tools as at 31 May 19X9 (inclusive of purchases during the year) were valued at £1,450.

The following additional valuations are available:

as at . . .	1 June 19X8 £	31 May 19X9 £
Subscriptions in arrears	278	220
Subscriptions in advance	90	135
Owing to suppliers of regalia	228	371
Stocks of regalia, at cost	255	298

▶**Task 1**

Draw up a summary Subscriptions Account for the year ended 31 May 19X9.

▶**Task 2**

Prepare a Trading Account for sales of regalia for the year ended 31 May 19X9.

▶**Task 3**

Prepare an Income and Expenditure Account for the club for the year ended 31 May 19X9.

Association of Accounting Technicians

SIMULATION 10

Capriol Club

Background information

You are the treasurer of the Capriol Club which encourages and promotes folk dancing. You have prepared the following analysis of bank and cash transactions for the year ended 31 October 19X2.

Capriol Club
Receipts and Payments Account for the year ended 31 October 19X2

	£		£
Cash and bank balances c/f	1,400	Secretarial expenses	578
Members' subscriptions	2,321	Rent	1,800
Donations	940	Visiting speakers' expenses	1,070
Sales of Annual Rally tickets	670	Donation to National Association	210
		Prizes for Annual Rally	365
		Other costs of Annual Rally	110
		Stationery and printing	421
		Cash and bank balances c/f	777
	5,331		5,331

The following additional information is also available:

(1) Members' subscriptions in arrears were £150 as at 1 November 19X1 and £184 as at 31 October 19X2. Subscriptions in advance were £36 at 1 November 19X1 and £168 at 31 October 19X2

(2) Amounts owing to suppliers of prizes for the Annual Rally were £12 at 1 November 19X1 and £54 at 31 October 19X2. Stocks of rally prizes in hand were £45 at 1 November 19X1 and £38 at 31 October 19X2

(3) The Capriol Club owns equipment which cost £3,680 and which was valued at £2,897 at 1 November 19X1 and £2,150 at 31 October 19X2

▶**Task 1**

Calculate the Accumulated Fund of the Capriol Club as at 1 November 19X1.

▶**Task 2**

Prepare the Income and Expenditure Account of the club for the year ended 31 October 19X2 bringing out the surplus or deficit on the Annual Rally.

▶**Task 3**

Prepare the Capriol Club's Balance Sheet as at 31 October 19X2.

Association of Accounting Technicians

Academicals Society

Background information

The treasurer of the Academicals Society has supplied you with the following summary of the society's cash and bank transactions for the year ended 31 May 19X1:

Receipts and Payments Account for the year ended 31 May 19X1

	£		£
Members' subscriptions	6,220	Balance b/f	950
Sales of conference tickets	3,260	Secretarial expenses	1,450
Balance c/f	1,340	Rent	2,000
		Visiting speakers' expenses	2,800
		Donations to charities	570
		Conference expenses	770
		Purchase of office equipment	1,650
		Stationery and printing	630
	10,820		10,820

The treasurer has also provided you with the following valuations:

	1 June 19X0	31 May 19X1
	£	£
Office equipment	3,480	4,385
Subscriptions in arrears	140	120
Subscriptions in advance	70	100
Accrued stationery and printing	260	350

The cost of the office equipment owned by the society as at 1 June 19X0 was £5,800.

It is estimated that 60% of the visiting speakers' expenses is attributable to the society's annual conference.

▶**Task 1**

Prepare the Academicals Society's Income and Expenditure Account for the year ended 31 May 19X1 showing clearly the surplus or deficit on the annual conference.

▶**Task 2**

Prepare the Academicals Society's Balance Sheet as at 31 May 19X1.

Association of Accounting Technicians

SIMULATION 12

Phoenix Model Engineering Society

Background information

The following account has been prepared by the treasurer of the Phoenix Model Engineering Society:

Receipts and payments statement for the year ended 31 March 19X9

	£		£
1 April 19X8 Opening balance b/fwd	894	Purchase of building land	8.000
Subscriptions received	12,000	Purchase of machinery and tools	17,500
Sales of machinery and tools	21,000	Rent of temporary office and meeting room	600
Sale of wooden hut	1,100	Printing, stationery and postages	860
Sales of tickets for annual national exhibition	300	Deposit in building society investment account	7,500
		Secretary's honorarium	150
		Coach to annual national exhibition	110
		Admission charges to annual national exhibition	220
		31 March 19X9 closing balance c/fwd	354
	£35,294		£35,294

The following additional information has been obtained from the Society's records:

(1) In addition to the balances at bank shown in the above receipts and payments statement, the Society's assets and liabilities were:

As at	1 April 19X8 £	31 March 19X9 £
Stocks of machinery and tools at cost	1,200	600
Subscriptions due to the Society	150	250
Wooden hut at valuation	1,300	–
Subscriptions prepaid by members	300	To be determined
Outing to annual national exhibition	–	See note 4 below

(2) The annual subscription for the year ended 31 March has been £50 per member since 1 April 19X7.

All subscriptions due at 1 April 19X8 have now been paid.

The Society's membership was 238 during the year ended 31 March 19X9.

(3) All sales of machinery and tools are to members on a strictly cash basis.

(4) *Annual National Exhibition*, £40 for tickets was owing by a member to the Society on 31 March 19X9 and at that date the Society owed £45 for the purchase of exhibition programmes distributed to members without charge.

(5) Since preparing the above receipts and payments statement, the treasurer has received a bank statement showing bank charges of £14 debited in the Society's bank account on 30 March 19X9; no adjustment was made for these charges in the above statement.

(6) Since the sale of the wooden hut on 1 July 19X8, the Society has rented a temporary office and meeting room at an annual rent of £600 payable in advance.

▶**Task**

Prepare an Income and Expenditure Account for the year ended 31 March 19X9 and a Balance Sheet as at that date for the Society.

Note: The Income and Expenditure Account should show clearly the overall result of the trade in machinery and tools and the profit or loss of the visit to the annual national exhibition.

Association of Accounting Technicians

SIMULATION 13^A

High Towers Rural Pursuits Society

Background information

The following receipts and payments account for the year ended 31 March 19X1 of the High Towers Rural Pursuits Society has been prepared by the society's treasurer John Higham.

	£	£
1 April 19X0 Balance brought forward		1,347
Receipts:		
Membership subscriptions:		
For the year ended 31 March 19X0	252	
For the year ended 31 March 19X1	6,810	
For the year ended 31 March 19X2	330	
	7,392	
Sale of photographic equipment	28,100	
Sale of small transit coach	2,560	38,052
		39,399
Payments:		
Purchase of photographic equipment	22,734	
Lecturer for rural hobbies course	460	
Purchase of land for proposed new meeting room and office	10,000	
Bank investment deposit account	3,000	
Stationery and postages	600	
Printing year book	810	
Advertising for new members	230	
National Society affiliation fee	180	
Meeting room hire	340	
Secretary's honorarium	300	38,654
31 March 19X1 Balance carried forward		£745

Additional information:

(1) The Society has a policy of not accounting for subscriptions until received.

(2) In addition to the items mentioned previously, the Society's assets and liabilities as at 1 April 19X0 were as follows:

	£
Stock of photographic equipment for resale, at cost	3,420
Subscriptions for the year ended 31 March 19X1 received prior to 31 March 19X0	420
Small transit coach at cost bought 1 April 19X6	18,000
Video equipment bought 31 March 19X0	1,200

Notes:

(i) When bought by the Society, the small transit coach was expected to be in use by the Society for five years and have a nil residual value.

(ii) The video equipment is expected to be in use by the Society until 31 March 19X4 when its residual value is expected to be £200.

(iii) The Society uses the straight line basis when providing for depreciation.

(3) All receipts and payments are passed through the Society's bank current account.

(4) The Society buys photographic equipment for sale to members on a cash basis at favourable prices; the photographic equipment in stock at 31 March 19X1 has been valued, at cost, at £1,800.

Members have requested that the Society's annual accounts should show the profit or loss arising from the sale of photographic equipment.

(5) The Society's bank investment deposit account was credited with interest of £82 on 31 March 19X1.

(6) The Society has now decided that an Income and Expenditure Account for the year ended 31 March 19X1 and a Balance Sheet as at that date should be prepared.

▶**Task**

Prepare the Society's Income and Expenditure Account for the year ended 31 March 19X1 and a Balance Sheet as at that date.

Association of Accounting Technicians

Local Amateur Dramatic Society

Unit 5
Preparing Financial Accounts
Element 5.1
Record income and expenditure Performance criteria **a b c d e**

Background information

The treasurer of the local amateur dramatic society, of which you are a member, has reported that the society has made a healthy surplus for the year to 30 June 19X0. He supports this statement by pointing to the fact that the cash in the society's current account at the bank has risen by £1,100, from £320 to £1,420, as shown in the following summary of receipts and payment which he has prepared:

Receipts	£	Payments	£
Balance brought down	320	Hire of halls	300
Subscriptions	1,000	Purchases of refreshments	
Box office takings	4,500	for resale	1,500
Transfer from deposit		Royalty payments for	
account	2,000	performance rights	2,500
Interest on deposit		Purchase of lighting,	
account	200	scenery and costumes	3,000
Sales of refreshments	2,300	Incidental expenses	1,600
		Balance carried down	1,420
	10,320		10,320

You wonder whether the treasurer's optimism is justified, and ascertain that the following balances existed at the start and end of the year:

	At 30 June 19X9 £	At 30 June 19X0 £
Creditors for purchases of refreshments	50	350
Deposit account	2,000	0
Lighting, scenery and costumes at written down value	10,000	To be calculated
Royalties prepaid	500	300

The annual charge for depreciation of scenery, lighting and costumes should be calculated as 20% of the written down balance brought forward plus any additions during the year.

There were no stocks and no subscriptions in advance or arrears at the start or end of the year.

▶ **Task 1**

Calculate the value of the society's accumulated fund at 30 June 19X9.

▶ **Task 2**

Prepare the Income and Expenditure Account of the society for the year to 30 June 19X0 and its Balance Sheet at that date.

▶**Task 3** To what extent do you agree with the treasurer that the society's financial progress during the year has been satisfactory?

Chartered Institute of Bankers

Mary Grimes

Background information

Mary Grimes, retail fruit and vegetable merchant, does not keep a full set of accounting records. However, the following information has been produced from the business's records:

1 Summary of the bank account for the year ended 31 August 19X8

	£		£
1 September 19X7 balance brought forward	1,970	Payments to suppliers	72,000
Receipts from trade debtors	96,000	Purchase of motor van (E471 KBR)	13,000
Sale of private yacht	20,000	Rent and rates	2,600
Sale of motor van (A123 BWA)	2,100	Wages	15,100
		Motor vehicle expenses	3,350
		Postages and stationery	1,360
		Drawings	9,200
		Repairs and renewals	650
		Insurances	800
		31 August 19X8 balance carried forward	2,010
	£120,070		£120,070
Balance b/f	2,010		

Notes:
(1) Assets and liabilities, other than balance at bank:

As at	1 September 19X7 £	31 August 19X8 £
Trade creditors	4,700	2,590
Trade debtors	7,320	9,500
Rent and rates accruals	200	260
Motor vans:		
A123 BWA – At cost	10,000	–
Provision for depreciation	8,000	–
E471 KBR – At cost	–	13,000
Provision for depreciation	–	To be determined
Stock in trade	4,900	5,900
Insurances prepaid	160	200

(2) All receipts are banked and all payments are made from the business bank account.

(3) A trade debt of £300 owing by John Blunt and included in the trade debtors at 31 August 19X8 (see 1 above), is to be written off as a bad debt.

(4) It is Mary Grimes' policy to provide depreciation at the rate of 20% on the cost of motor vans held at the end of each financial year; no depreciation is provided in the year of sale or disposal of a motor van.

(5) Discounts received during the year ended 31 August 19X8 from trade creditors amounted to £1,100.

▶Task 1

Prepare Mary Grimes' Trading and Profit and Loss Account for the year ended 31 August 19X8.

▶Task 2

Prepare Mary Grimes' Balance Sheet as at 31 August 19X8.

Association of Accounting Technicians

See Step-by-Step Guide to Incomplete Records, page 24.

SIMULATION 16

Jane Brandon

Unit 5
Preparing Financial Accounts
Element 5.2
Prepare accounts from incomplete records
Performance criteria **a b c d e f**

Background information

The following is a summary of the bank account of Jane Brandon, a retailer, for the year ended 31 March 19X9.

	£		£
Balance b/d 1.4.X8	16,420	Payments to creditors	46,212
Receipts from debtors	68,947	Rent	2,641
		Rates	1,217
		Drawings	10,928
		Sundry expenses	3,796
		Loan repayments	2,000
		Balance c/d 31.3.X9	18,573
	85,367		85,367

A list of assets and liabilities at 31 March 19X8 has been provided:

Assets	£
Freehold premises	66,069
Fixtures and fittings at net book value (original cost £10,500)	8,450
Trade debtors	5,352
Stock	10,216
Rent prepaid	142
Bank	16,420
	106,649
Liabilities	
Trade creditors	4,181
Loan	45,000
	49,181

Other information relating to the business is as follows:

(1) Fixtures and fittings are depreciated at 10% per annum on cost.
(2) On 31 March 19X9 £150 is owing for rent.
(3) At 31 March 19X9:

	£
Stock	11,442
Trade debtors	4,825
Trade creditors	4,430

▶**Task**

Prepare Jane Brandon's Trading and Profit and Loss Account for the year ended 31 March 19X9 and her Balance Sheet at 31 March 19X9.

Association of Accounting Technicians

David's Fruiterer

Unit 5
Preparing Financial Accounts
Element 5.2
Prepare accounts from incomplete records
Performance criteria **a b c d e f**

Background information

David owns a fruiterer's shop and his annual accounting date is 30 September. David's balance sheet at 30 September 19X8 was as follows:

Balance Sheet as at 30 September 19X8

	£	£
Leasehold shop at cost	12,100	
Less Depreciation	8,150	
		3,950
Shop equipment at cost	19,634	
Less Depreciation	11,585	
		8,049
		11,999
Stock	931	
Trade debtors	358	
Deposit account	6,412	
	7,701	
Less		
Trade creditors	2,150	
Bank overdraft	32	
	2,182	
		5,519
		17,518
Financed by		
Capital account		17,518

David's bank account for the year to 30 September 19X9 may be summarised as follows:

Bank Current Account

	£		£
Takings paid to bank	60,205	Balance 1 October 19X8	32
Interest on deposit account	428	Payments to suppliers	37,014
		Wages	10,398
		Rent and rates	7,500
		Heating and lighting	1,201
		Bank charges	314
		Transfer to bank deposit account	500
		Sundry trade expenses	1,792
		Personal drawings	1,047
		Balance 30 September 19X9	835
	60,633		60,633

Other information relating to the year ended 30 September 19X9 is given below.

(1) All cash takings had been paid into the bank with the exception of £5,500 which David withheld for personal expenditure.

(2) At 30 September 19X9 stock was valued at £1,240; debtors amounted to £241; David owed his suppliers £786.

(3) Depreciation to be charged for the year is to be £1,210 in respect of the leasehold shop, and £1,422 in respect of the shop equipment.

(4) At 30 September 19X9 rent and rates were prepaid by £824, and electricity charges accrued were £210.

▶**Task 1**   Prepare a Trading and Profit and Loss Account for the year ended 30 September 19X9.

▶**Task 2**   Prepare a Balance Sheet at 30 September 19X9.

Chartered Institute of Bankers

SIMULATION 18

Unit 5
Preparing Financial Accounts
Element 5.2
Prepare accounts from incomplete records Performance criteria **a b c d e f**

Barry's Taxi

Background information

Barry is a taxi-driver who owns his taxi. It cost £10,500 new when he commenced business on 1st May 19X6, he is using the reducing balance method of depreciation at 25% p.a.

At 30 April 19X7, he had prepaid expenses of £453 in respect of the licence and insurance on his vehicle, he was owed £312 for fares incurred by regular customers (with whom he operates a monthly account) and in turn owed a garage £209 for servicing and petrol.

At 30 April 19X8, his prepaid expenses on licence and insurance amount to £531, his regular customers owe him £587, and his debt to the garage is £319.

A summary of his bank account for the year ended 30 April 19X8 is given below:

Summary Bank Account

	£		£
Balance b/fwd	34	Taxi operating expenses	10,317
Bankings	16,013	Hire of two-way radio	540
Advertising revenue		Advertising in telephone	
from roof sign	200	directory	192
		Trade subscription	75
		Supply and fitting of illuminated roof sign to carry advertisements	520
		Bank charges	48
		Foreign currency (for Dutch holiday)	427
		Personal expenses (including mortgage payments on house, income tax, rates)	3,147
		Balance c/fwd	981
	£16,247		£16,247

The bankings represented all monies received for fares (including tips) after £75 per week for each of 50 weeks had been deducted: the latter sum he has retained in cash for housekeeping and personal expenses.

▶**Task 1**

Prepare a Balance Sheet at 30 April 19X7.

▶**Task 2**

Prepare a Profit and Loss Account for the year ended 30 April 19X8.

▶Task 3

Prepare a Balance sheet at 30 April 19X8.

Chartered Institute of Bankers (amended)

SIMULATION 19^A

Unit 5
Preparing Financial Accounts
Element 5.2
Prepare accounts from incomplete records Performance criteria **a b c d e f**

Jane Simpson

Background information

Jane Simpson, a retail trader, has been trying to keep her own accounting records and has extracted the following list of balances as at 30 April 19X9 from her accounts prior to the preparation of the annual accounts and balance sheet by James Lang, an accounting technician:

	£
Fixtures and fittings:	
at cost	8,000
provision for depreciation at 1 May 19X8	3,000
Motor vehicles:	
at cost	9,600
provision for depreciation at 1 May 19X8	5,600
Stock in trade	12,000
Trade debtors	7,000
Balance at bank	1,700
Trade creditors	6,900
Sales	132,000
Cost of sales	79,200
Establishment and administrative expenses	11,800
Sales and distribution expenses	33,500
Drawings	9,700
Capital	30,000

In preparing the annual accounts, James Lang made the following discoveries:

(1) The Trial Balance as at 30 April 19X9 prepared from the above list of balances did not balance.

(2) The stock in trade at 30 April 19X8 should have been valued at £16,000 not £13,000 as included in the accounts for the year ended 30 April 19X8.

(3) Provision is to be made for a commission for sales staff of 2% of gross profit in the accounts for the year ended 30 April 19X9.

(4) An entry in the cash book for the purchase of fixtures and fittings on 1 February 19X9 costing £4,500 has not been posted to the ledger.

(5) Depreciation is to be provided for the year ended 30 April 19X9 as follows:
Fixtures and fittings   10% per annum on cost;
Motor vehicles   25% per annum on cost.

(6) A credit sale of £4,700 in March 19X9 was included correctly in the posting to the sales account, but recorded as £4,200 in the debtor's account.

(7) Goods costing £600 withdrawn by Jane Simpson for her own use have not been recorded in the accounts.

▶**Task 1**   Prepare Jane Simpson's uncorrected Trial Balance as at 30 April 19X9.

▶Task 2

Prepare Jane Simpson's Trading and Profit and Loss Account for the year ended 30 April 19X9 and Balance Sheet as at that date.

Association of Accounting Technicians

SIMULATION 20

Unit 5
Preparing Financial Accounts
Element 5.2
Prepare accounts from incomplete records
Performance criteria **a b c d e f**

Pat's Card & Gift Shop

Background information

Pat operates a card/gift shop which she formed two years ago, by borrowing £10,000 from her father who agreed to accept interest at a nominal 6% per annum. The repayment of the loan has been deferred until some later date when Pat's business has become established.

Unfortunately, Pat has been unable to keep proper records but she has been able to supply the following details.

(a) Below is a summary of all her payments made during the year ended 31st December 19X0 from her bank statements:

	£
Rates	630
Insurance	1,300
Payments to suppliers (including £3,350 paid to creditors for previous year)	25,250
Loan interest	550
Drawings	8,000
Motor expenses	670
Wages paid to shop assistants	8,000
Purchase of new display stand	2,000
Sundry expenses	360
Electricity	625
Rent of shop	5,600
Telephone	200

At the start of the year, 1st January 19X0, Pat had Cash at Bank amounting to £4,100.

(b) During the year Pat's takings totalled £56,000.

(c) All her sales of cards and gifts have been arrived at by allowing a 60% profit margin on her selling price.

(d) The display equipment is subject to depreciation at 15% per annum and the Motor Car 20% per annum on the cost price of the assets held at the end of the year. The Balance Sheet as at 31st December 19X9 included the following:

	Cost	Aggregate Depreciation	Net Book Value
	£	£	£
Display equipment	8,600	1,290	7,310
Motor car	8,000	1,600	6,400

(e) At the end of 31st December 19X0 Pat still had to settle her telephone bill which amounted to £48 and her local garage bill for petrol which was £73.

▶ Task 1

Calculate Pat's opening capital as at 1st January 19X0.

▶ Task 2

From the information given you are required to compute Pat's bank balance as at 31st December 19X0.

▶ Task 3

Prepare a Trading and Profit and Loss Account for the year ended 31st December 19X0 and a Balance Sheet as at that date.

SIMULATION 21^A

S. Thorn

Background information

Trial Balance of S. Thorn as at 31 January 19X3

	Dr	Cr
	£	£
Capital		19,420
Equipment	3,750	
Furniture & fittings	2,000	
Motor vehicle	5,790	
Sales		32,010
Purchases	19,740	
Bank	250	
General expenses	600	
Wages	5,940	
Rent, rates and insurance	2,550	
Heating and lighting	700	
Debtors	8,000	
Creditors		3,600
Stock 1st February 19X2	5,710	
	55,030	55,030

Notes:

(a) Closing stock at 31st January 19X3 was £4,910.

(b) Heating and lighting expenses owing at 31st January 19X3 amounted to £117.

(c) Rent prepaid was £200.

▶ **Task 1**

Prepare an Extended Trial Balance for S. Thorn as at 31st January 19X3 showing clearly the gross and net profit for the year.

▶ **Task 2**

Prepare a Trading and Profit and Loss Account for the year ended 31st January 19X3 and a Balance Sheet at that date.

SIMULATION 22

Ramsey

Background information

The following figures have been extracted from the books of Ramsey as at 31 December 19X8:

Trial balance as at 31 December 19X8

	Dr	Cr
	£	£
Capital		24,860
Sales		94,360
Purchases	48,910	
Fixed assets at cost	32,750	
Provision for depreciation		11,500
Debtors	17,190	
Bank	18,100	
Creditors		11,075
Stock 1.1.19X8	8,620	
Rent	4,200	
Electricity	2,150	
Drawings	9,875	
	141,795	141,795

The following additional information is provided:

(1) The stock at 31.12.19X8 is £9,180.

(2) Depreciation for the year is to be charged at 10% of the cost of the fixed assets.

(3) Rent of £300 is prepaid for 19X9.

(4) Electricity of £250 is still owing on 31.12.19X8.

▶**Task 1**

Prepare an Extended Trial Balance for Ramsey as at 31 December 19X8 showing clearly the profit for the year.

▶**Task 2**

Prepare a Trading and Profit and Loss Account for the year ended 31st December 19X8 and a Balance Sheet at that date.

Association of Accounting Technicians

D.J. Lindhurst

Background information

The following Trial Balance was extracted from the books of D.J. Lindhurst a retailer selling electrical goods.

Trial Balance of D.J. Lindhurst as at 31st December 199X

	Dr	Cr
	£	£
Purchases	73,936	
Sales		101,230
Carriage inwards	245	
Carriage outwards	703	
Returns inwards & outwards	212	1,140
Stock (1st January 199X)	4,910	
Wages & salaries	14,975	
Rent, rates & insurance	2,950	
Heating & lighting	627	
Motor vehicle	4,500	
Motor expenses	1,250	
Capital (1st January 199X)		18,948
Bank overdraft		2,819
Furniture & fittings	3,200	
Drawings	13,950	
Debtors	11,600	
Creditors		8,921
	133,058	133,058

Notes:
(a) Stock at 31st December 199X was valued at £6,021.
(b) Rent owing at 31st December 199X was £220.
(c) Rates paid in advance amounted to £180.
(d) Depreciate the motor vehicle at 20% on cost.

▶ **Task 1**

Prepare an Extended Trial Balance at 31st December 199X.

▶ **Task 2**

Prepare a Trading and Profit and Loss Account for the year ended 31st December 199X and a Balance Sheet as at that date.

SIMULATION 24

Stephen Chee

Background information

The following Trial Balance was extracted from the ledger of Stephen Chee a sole trader, as 31 May 19X0 – the end of his financial year.

Stephen Chee
Trial Balance as at 31 May 19X0

	Dr	Cr
	£	£
Property, at cost	120,000	
Equipment at cost	80,000	
Provisions for depreciation (as at 1 June 19X9)		
on property		20,000
on equipment		38,000
Purchases	250,000	
Sales		402,200
Stock, as at 1 June 19X9	50,000	
Discounts allowed	18,000	
Discounts received		4,800
Returns out		15,000
Wages and salaries	58,800	
Bad debts	4,600	
Loan interest	5,100	
Other operating expenses	17,700	
Trade creditors		36,000
Trade debtors	38,000	
Cash in hand	300	
Bank	1,300	
Drawings	24,000	
Provision for bad debts		500
17% Long term loan		30,000
Capital, as at 1 June 19X9		121,300
	667,800	667,800

The following information as at 31 May 19X0 is available:

(a) Stock as at the close of business has been valued at cost at £42,000.

(b) Wages and salaries are accrued by £800.

(c) Other operating expenses are prepaid by £300.

(d) The provision for bad debts is to be adjusted so that it is 2% of trade debtors.

(e) Depreciation for the year ended 31 May 19X0 has still to be provided for as follows:

Property – 1.5% per annum using the straight line method, and
Equipment – 25% per annum using the diminishing balance method.

▶ **Task 1**

Prepare an Extended Trial Balance for Stephen Chee as at 31st May 19X0 showing clearly the gross and net profits for the year.

▶ **Task 2**

Prepare Stephen Chee's Trading and Profit and Loss Account for the year ended 31st May 19X0 and his Balance Sheet as at that date.

Association of Accounting Technicians
(adjusted to include Extended Trial Balance)

SIMULATION 25

Mr Banda

Background information

The following is a list of balances taken from the ledger of Mr Banda, a sole trader, as at 31 July 19X6 – the end of his most recent financial year.

List of Balances as at 31 July 19X6

	£
Stock at 1 August 19X5	5,830
Plant and machinery	
at cost	36,420
accumulated depreciation	14,568
Purchases	48,760
Sales	101,890
Discounts allowed	1,324
Discounts received	1,150
Returns to suppliers	531
Returns from customers	761
Wages and salaries	15,300
Other operating expenses	21,850
Trade creditors	4,380
Trade debtors	6,340
Cash in hand	199
Cash at bank	2,197
Drawings	8,465
Capital	24,927

The following additional information as at 31 July 19X6 is available:

(a) Stock at the close of business was valued at £6,140.

(b) Certain operating expenses have been prepaid by £172 and others have been accrued by £233.

(c) Plant and machinery has still to be depreciated for 19X6 at 20% per annum on cost.

(d) Other operating expenses include the following:

	£
Carriage inwards	650
Carriage outwards	1,540

▶**Task 1**

Prepare an Extended Trial Balance for the year ended 31 July 19X6.

▶**Task 2**

Prepare for Mr Banda's business a Trading and Profit and Loss Account for the year ended 31 July 19X6 and a Balance Sheet as at that date.

Association of Accounting Technicians

Stamper

Background information

The following is the Trial Balance extracted from the ledger of Stamper, a sole trader who runs a shop, at 31 December 19X9:

	£	£
Capital 1 January 19X9		52,500
Drawings	20,000	
Sales		150,750
Purchases	112,800	
Stock at 1 January 19X9	25,600	
Wages	12,610	
Rent	2,500	
Motor expenses	1,240	
Motor vehicle: at cost	17,000	
accumulated depreciation at 1 January 19X9		3,000
Equipment: at cost	15,000	
accumulated depreciation at 1 January 19X9		4,500
Bank	900	
Debtors	9,950	
Creditors		8,100
Cash float	250	
Insurance	1,000	
	218,850	218,850

You are given the following additional information:

(1) Stock at 31 December 19X9 was valued at £27,350.

(2) Rent of £500 (included in the figure of £2,500 above) was prepaid at 31 December 19X9.

(3) Motor expenses of £140 are to be accrued at 31 December 19X9.

(4) A bad debt of £200 is to be written off.

(5) An invoice for insurance of £450 was wrongly recorded as purchases, and is included under purchases in the Trial Balance.

(6) The motor vehicle is depreciated on the straight line basis assuming a life of four years and a residual value of £5,000; the equipment is depreciated on the reducing balance basis using an annual rate of 30%.

▶**Task**

Prepare the Trading and Profit and Loss Account of Stamper for the year to 31 December 19X9 and the Balance Sheet at that date.

Chartered Institute of Bankers

Andrew Pye

Background information

The following Trial Balance has been extracted from the ledger of Andrew Pye, a sole trader, as at 31 October 19X8, the end of Mr Pye's financial year.

Trial Balance as at 31 October 19X8

	Dr £	Cr £
Stock, as at 1 November 19X7	22,000	
Purchases	223,000	
Sales		340,700
Discounts allowed	4,600	
Discounts received		5,500
Returns in	6,700	
Returns out		5,600
Wages and salaries	34,500	
Bad debts	3,100	
Carriage in	1,400	
Carriage out	2,200	
Other operating expenses	24,500	
Trade debtors	34,000	
Trade creditors		21,600
Provisions for bad debts		450
Cash in hand	800	
Bank overdraft		23,400
Drawings	23,500	
Capital, as at 1 November 19X7		62,050
Property	50,000	
Equipment	64,000	
Provisions for depreciation (as at 1 November 19X7)		
property		10,000
equipment		25,000
	494,300	494,300

The following additional information as at 31 October 19X8 is available:

(1) Stock as at the close of business was valued at £23,700.

(2) 'Other operating expenses' were prepaid by £170.

(3) The provision for bad debts is to be adjusted so that it is 1% of trade debtors.

(4) Depreciation had still to be provided for the year ended 31 October 19X8 as follows:
  Property – 2% straight line method
  Equipment – 30% diminishing balance method.

Prepare Andrew Pye's Trading and Profit and Loss Account for the year ended 31 October 19X8 and his Balance Sheet as at 31 October 19X8.

Association of Accounting Technicians

	Unit 5
	Preparing Financial Accounts

Herbert Howell

The following Trial Balance has been extracted from the ledger of Herbert Howell, a sole trader, as at 31 May 19X9, the end of his most recent financial year:

Trial Balance as at 31 May 19X9

	Dr £	Cr £
Property, at cost	90,000	
Equipment, at cost	57,500	
Provisions for depreciation (as at 1 June 19X8)		
property		12,500
equipment		32,500
Stock, as at 1 June 19X8	27,400	
Purchases	259,600	
Sales		405,000
Discounts allowed	3,370	
Discounts received		4,420
Wages and salaries	52,360	
Bad debts	1,720	
Loan interest	1,560	
Carriage out	5,310	
Other operating expenses	38,800	
Trade debtors	46,200	
Trade creditors		33,600
Provision for bad debts		280
Cash in hand	151	
Bank overdraft		14,500
Drawings	28,930	
13% Loan		12,000
Capital, as at 1 June 19X8		98,101
	612,901	612,901

The following additional information as at 31 May 19X9 is available:

(a) Stock as at the close of business was valued at £25,900.

(b) Depreciation for the year ended 31 May 19X9 has yet to be provided as follows:
    Property – 1% using the straight line method.
    Equipment – 15% using the straight line method.

(c) Wages and salaries are accrued by £140.

(d) 'Other operating expenses' includes certain expenses prepaid by £500. Other expenses included under this heading are accrued by £200.

(e) The provision for bad debts is to be adjusted so that it is 0.5% of trade debtors as at 31 May 19X9.

(f) 'Purchases' includes goods valued at £1,040 which were withdrawn by Mr Howell for his own personal use.

▶**Task**   Prepare Mr Howell's Trading and Profit and Loss Account for the year ended 31 May 19X9 and his Balance Sheet as at 31 May 19X9.

Association of Accounting Technicians

Recording Cost Information

> **Elements**
> 6.1 Operate and maintain a system of accounting for material costs
> 6.2 Operate and maintain a system of accounting for labour costs
> 6.3 Operate and maintain a system of accounting for expenses
> 6.4 Operate and maintain a system for the apportionment and absorption of indirect costs (overheads)

Standards of Competence

ELEMENT 6.1 OPERATE AND MAINTAIN A SYSTEM OF ACCOUNTING FOR MATERIAL COSTS

Performance Criteria

a Data are correctly coded, analysed and recorded
b Standard costs for materials are established in accordance with the organisation's procedures
c Materials issued from stores are correctly priced in accordance with the organisation's policy
d Materials issued are systematically checked against the organisation's overall usage and stock control practices and unusual issues reported to management
e Timely information on materials usage is accurately presented to management
f Any queries are either resolved immediately or referred to the appropriate person

Range Statement

- Materials issued from stores within the organisation
- Standard and actual material costs
- Direct and indirect materials costs

Knowledge and Understanding

The business environment
- Main types of materials: (see Range Statement)

Accounting techniques
- Methods of stock control
- Methods of materials pricing: (see Range Statement)
- Basic analysis of variances: usage, price
- Procedures for establishing standard materials costs, use of technical and purchasing information
- Purchasing procedures and documentation
- Methods of analysing materials usage: reasons for wastage

Accounting principles and theory
- Relationship between technical systems and costing systems – job, batch, unit, process costing systems
- Principles of standard costing systems: variance reports
- Relationships between the materials costing system and the stock control system

The organisation
Background understanding that the accounting systems of an organisation are affected by its organisational structure, its administrative systems and procedures and the nature of its business transactions

ELEMENT 6.2 OPERATE AND MAINTAIN A SYSTEM OF ACCOUNTING FOR LABOUR COSTS

Performance Criteria

a Data are correctly coded, analysed and recorded

b Standard labour costs are established in accordance with the organisation's procedures

c Labour costs are calculated in accordance with the organisation's policies and procedures

d Timely information relating to labour utilisation is presented accurately to management

e Staff working in operational departments are consulted to resolve any queries in the data

Range Statement

• Employees of the organisation on the payroll. Self employed persons excluded

• Labour costs: salaried labour, payment by results, time rates

• Standard and actual labour costs

• Direct and indirect labour costs

Knowledge and Understanding

The business environment
• Methods of payment for employees

Accounting techniques
• Procedures for establishing standard labour costs: use of work study information and information about labour rates
• Basic analysis of variances: rate, utilisation
• Analysis of labour utilisation: idle time, overtime, levels, absenteeism, sickness rates

Accounting principles and theory
• Relationship between technical systems and costing systems – job, batch, unit, process costing systems
• Principles of standard costing systems: variance reports
• Relationships between the labour costing system and the payroll accounting system

The organisation
Background understanding that the accounting systems of an organisation are affected by its organisational structure, its administrative systems and procedures and the nature of its business transactions

ELEMENT 6.3 OPERATE AND MAINTAIN A SYSTEM OF ACCOUNTING FOR EXPENSES

Performance Criteria

a Data are correctly coded, analysed and recorded

b Standard costs for expenses are established in accordance with the organisation's procedures

c Information relating to expenses is accurately and clearly presented to management

d Staff working in operational departments are consulted to resolve any queries in the data

Range Statement

• Expenses: revenue and capital expenditure invoiced to the organisation, depreciation charges

• Actual and standard costs for expenses

[Note that this element is concerned with the initial recording of the expenses. Reallocation (as part of overhead apportionment/absorption is covered in 6.4)]

The business environment
- Main types of expenses: expenses directly charged to cost units (e.g. subcontracting charges), indirect expense, depreciation charges

Accounting techniques
- Methods of setting standards for expenses
- Basic analysis of variances: usage, price
- Procedures and documentation relating to expenses
- Allocation of expenses to cost centres

Accounting principles and theory
- Relationship between technical systems and costing systems – job, batch, unit, process costing systems
- Principles of standard costing systems: variance reports
- Relationships between the expenses costing system and the accounting system
- Objectives of depreciation accounting

The organisation
Background understanding that the accounting systems of an organisation are affected by its organisational structure, its administrative systems and procedures and the nature of its business transactions

ELEMENT 6.4   OPERATE AND MAINTAIN A SYSTEM FOR THE APPORTIONMENT AND ABSORPTION OF INDIRECT COSTS (OVERHEADS)

a   Overhead costs are correctly attributed to direct cost centres and cost units in accordance with agreed methods of apportionment and absorption

b   Adjustments for under/over recorded overheads are made in accordance with established procedures

c   Methods of overhead apportionment and absorption are reviewed at regular intervals in discussion with senior staff

d   Staff working in operational departments are consulted to resolve any queries in the data

- Indirect costs (overheads) which need to be attributed to cost centres/cost units – indirect materials, indirect labour and indirect expenses
- Methods of apportionment: floor area, number of employees, time taken, use of service

Accounting techniques
- Calculation of overhead variances: capacity variances
- Procedures for establishing standard absorption rates (see Range Statement)
- Bases of apportioning indirect costs to responsibility centres
- Activity based systems of allocating costs; cost drivers

Accounting principles and theory
- Relationship between technical systems and costing systems – job, batch, unit, process costing systems
- Principles of standard costing systems: variance reports
- Nature and significance of overhead costs: fixed costs and variable costs
- Effect of changes in capacity levels
- Arbitrary nature of overhead apportionments

The organisation
Background understanding that the accounting systems of an organisation are affected by its organisational structure, its administrative systems and procedures and the nature of its business transactions

Decor Designs

Background information

Andrew Dennis and Mark Conner had worked for a successful manufacturer of specialist kitchen and bedroom furniture for many years. They decided to start up in the same type of business and managed to rent a smaller unit on an industrial estate. They purchased some second-hand machinery for producing the fitted bedroom furniture but purchased the basic kitchen units and offered various designs of doors. Their company Decor Designs achieved consistently good sales but they realised that their quotations were hit and miss since they had no proper costing system. In fact, neither of them had much knowledge of costing so Andrew asked a relative of his who worked at the local college to help. As a first step they need to understand costing terms before deciding on a suitable system.

▶ **Task 1**

Prepare a reference booklet for Andrew and Mark of the terms normally used in costing. The explanation of the terms should be in a readily understandable form, and should include:

Cost centre
Cost unit
Direct material cost
Direct labour
Direct expenses
Indirect material cost
Indirect labour
Indirect expenses
Fixed costs
Variable costs
Stock control
Perpetual inventory
Methods of stock valuation
   – First In First Out
   – Last In First Out
   – Average cost method
   – Periodic weighted average pricing
   – Standard cost
   – Replacement cost
Overheads
   – Production
   – Administration
   – Selling and distribution
   – Allocation and apportionment
Remuneration methods

You may include anything else you feel will be useful to the partners.

This task may be carried out individually or in a group and ideally should be produced using a word-processing package.

Yates Country Supplies

Unit 6
Recording Cost Information
Element 6.1
Operate and maintain a system of accounting for material costs Performance criteria **a c e**

Background information

Yates Country Supplies is a stockist of agricultural gates and fencing. Their galvanised gates, 3 metres long, are in regular demand and they take delivery of these on a regular basis.

The firm's Stock Ledger Card for the 3 metre galvanised gate is as follows:

Date	RECEIPTS			ISSUES			BALANCE	
	QTY	PRICE	£'s	QTY	PRICE	£'s	QTY	£'s
January	20	£30						
March	20	£34						
April				16				
August	40	£40						
December				48				

Stock Ledger Card – 3m Galvanised Gates

▶**Task**

You are required to calculate the closing stock figure of the gates at the end of the financial year using the following bases:

(a) Last-In-First-Out
(b) First-In-First-Out
(c) Average cost method

Draw up your own ledger card.

MA & F

Sandover & Sons Ltd

Unit 6
Recording Cost Information
Element 6.1
Operate and maintain a system of accounting for material costs Performance criteria **a c e**

Background information

Sandover & Sons Ltd manufacture a single product and maintain a perpetual inventory. The stock records show a balance of 1,000 units in stock at the beginning of January 19X3 valued at a price of £7.50 each.

The following transactions took place during the six months ended 30th June 19X3. For record purposes the item produced is a metal container code reference TQ 5450.

January	–	Sold 750 units @ £16 each
February	–	Received 500 units @ £10 each
March	–	Sold 400 units @ £16 each
April	–	Received 750 units @ £10.40 each
May	–	Received 1,000 units @ £10.80 each
June	–	Sold 1,100 units @ £16.00 each

▶**Task 1**

Your task is to draw up a stock ledger record and calculate the stock valuation at 30th June 19X3 using:

(a) The LIFO Method

(b) The FIFO Method.

▶**Task 2**

To draw up a Trading Account for the six months from January to June 19X3 showing clearly the profit using both the LIFO and FIFO methods of stock valuation.

MA & F

SIMULATION 32^A

Mr Holder

Background information

Mr Holder is a wholesaler of stock which requires no further activity to prepare units for sale and the following is a record of his purchases and sales for June 19X2.

June 1st	Stock in hand	1,000 units @ £20
June 8th	Purchased	7,000 units @ £22
June 15th	Sold	5,000 units @ £30
June 18th	Purchased	4,000 units @ £24
June 22nd	Purchased	2,000 units @ £26
June 30th	Sold	5,000 units @ £35

▶**Task 1**

Compute the value of purchases and sales of these items for June 19X2.

▶**Task 2**

How many units should there be in stock at 30th June?

▶**Task 3**

Calculate the value of the stock at 30th June 19X2 using the following:

(a) FIFO

(b) LIFO

(c) AVCO.

▶**Task 4**

Using the three stock valuation figures obtained in Task 3 calculate the Gross Profit for the month of June 19X2.

Andrew Leck

Background information

Andrew Leck made the following purchases and sales of a certain stock item during the month of November 19X2:

8 Nov.	Purchased 16,000 units at £11.00 each
14 Nov.	Sold 10,000 units at £15.00 each
17 Nov.	Purchased 8,000 units at £12.00 each
20 Nov.	Purchased 4,000 units at £13.00 each
30 Nov.	Sold 10,000 units at £17.50 each

There were no stock items of this type as at 1 November 19X2.

▶ **Task 1**

Compute the values for Sales and Purchases of this stock item for November 19X2.

▶ **Task 2**

State how many units should there be in stock as at 30 November 19X2.

▶ **Task 3**

Value the units in stock as at 30 November 19X2 using each of the following bases:

(i)   FIFO

(ii)   LIFO

(iii) Average cost.

Association of Accounting Technicians

SIMULATION 34

P. Paul

Background information

P. Paul has been in business for three years, deals in only one product, and has used the FIFO method of valuing stock-in-trade on a perpetual inventory basis. The figures of receipts and sales are as follows:

		Receipts		*Sales*
Year 1	January	28 at £10 each	March	11 for £16 each
	April	12 at £10 each	August	15 for £16 each
	November	14 at £11 each	December	10 for £16.5 each
Year 2	February	9 at £12 each	April	17 for £17 each
	June	10 at £13 each	July	8 for £17 each
	August	8 at £12 each	December	30 for £19 each
	November	20 at £13 each		
Year 3	January	15 at £15 each	February	15 for £19 each
	April	10 at £16 each	November	32 for £22 each
	June	10 at £17 each		
	October	20 at £19 each		

▶Task 1

You are required to calculate the value of the stock in trade for each of the three years using:

(a) The FIFO basis

(b) The LIFO basis

(c) The AVCO basis.

▶Task 2

Prepare Trading Accounts for each of the three years assuming that the stock records were kept on a perpetual basis if:

(i)   the FIFO method had been used,

(ii) the LIFO method was used, and

(iii) the AVCO method was used.

SIMULATION 35^A

The Eclipse Valve Co.

Unit 6
Recording Cost Information
Element 6.1
Operate and maintain a system of accounting for material costs Performance criteria **a b c d e f**

Background information

The Eclipse Valve Co. was started four years ago by John Cooper an ex Technical Sales Engineer. The company stocks several products, one of which is a valve for use in the petrochemical industry. The bin card for this Item Code No. VX 4924 for the month of April is as follows:

ITEM – VALVE CODE NO. VX 4924			
Opening stock as at 1st April 180 units x £18			
Date	Receipts units	Price paid per unit	Issues unit
19X3		£	
April 3	360	17.70	
9			240
15	120	18.15	
20			240
27	60	18.60	
28			175
30	300	18.90	

▶**Task 1**

Complete a stores ledger card for stock item VX 4924 showing the value of the stock at 30th April using:

(a) First-In-First-Out Method of Valuation

(b) Last-In-First-Out Method of Valuation

(c) Cumulative Weighted Average Method.

▶**Task 2**

(a) Calculate the value of stock at 30th April using the Periodic Weighted Average Method.

(b) You are also requested to calculate the value of the stock at 30th April using the Standard Cost Method, for this purpose you are to assume that the standard cost price per unit is £18.00.

(c) Assuming the current average market price per unit was £18.00 on 1st April, rising to £18.15 on 9th April, £18.50 on 16th April and £18.90 on 30th April, calculate the value of the stock at 30th April using the Replacement Cost Method.

MA & F

(d) Indicate the difference between the purchase price and the aggregate of the cost of each batch of materials issued and the value of the closing stock at the 30th April for the following methods:

Standard Cost
and
Replacement Cost.

Kitchen Planners Ltd

Background information

Kitchen Planners Limited are distributors of the Summerday Kitchen Unit Type B670 which was marketed initially on 1 August 19X0. Up to 1 August 19X2, Kitchen Planners Limited were able to purchase the kitchen units at £1,050 each from any of its national manufacturers who operate under licences granted by the foreign designers. However, in recent months increased demand for the units coupled with some shortages of parts has resulted in a series of manufacturers' price increases.

In the absence of the departmental accountant overseas, a temporary member of the accounts staff has produced the following:

Summerday Kitchen Unit Type B670
Trading and Profit and Loss Account for the 4 months ended 30 November 19X2

	£	£
Sales		40,000
Cost of sales		13,350
Gross profit		26,650
Sales staff commission	2,665	
(10% of gross profit)		
Other variable overheads	12,000	
Fixed overheads	6,000	
		20,665
Net profit		5,985

It has now been discovered that the above statement is based on the last in, first out, (LIFO) method of stock valuation instead of first in, first out (FIFO), favoured by the company.

An irritated sales manager has observed that ultimately, whichever valuation method is used, the eventual overall gross profit is not changed.

Additional information:

(1) Purchases and sales of the Summerday Kitchen Unit Type B670 during the 4 months ended 30 November 19X2.

19X2	Purchases	Sales
5 August		2 units
10 September	3 units at £1,200 each	
18 September		4 units
25 September	5 units at £1,300 each	
8 October		3 units
11 November	2 units at £1,350 each	
20 November		2 units

(2) Three Summerday Units Type B670 were in stock on 30 November 19X2.

▶Task 1

Prepare a Trading and Profit and Loss Account for the 4 months ended 30 November 19X2 for the Summerday Kitchen Unit Type B670 based on the first in first out (FIFO) method of stock valuation.

Note: The opening and closing stock valuations should be shown.

▶Task 2

Draft a reasoned reply to the sales manager's observation.

Association of Accounting Technicians

Paul Bradley

Background information

Paul Bradley owns and runs an electrical contracting business in Stockport, Cheshire. He employs four skilled workers and ten unskilled workers. Much of his work is carried out on a sub-contractor basis to larger companies and for this reason he wishes to charge work out on an hourly basis.

▶**Task**

From the following information calculate a group labour hour rate assuming 52 weeks a year.

	Skilled worker	Unskilled worker
No. of employees	4	10
Hours worked (week)	50	50
Holidays per year	4 weeks on full pay	4 weeks on full pay
Idle time	5%	5%
Wage rate (per hour)	£6.00	£4.00
Lodging allowance (per week)	£100.00	£70.00
Food allowance (per week)	£50.00	£30.00

SIMULATION 38

Charles Meakin & Co.

Background information

Charles Meakin owns a small building contractors and employs three skilled bricklayers and two labourers. Most of the work is done as a subcontractor to large companies. He wishes to charge out the work done by his employees on an hourly basis.

▶Task

From the following information calculate a labour hour rate for the group assuming fifty-two weeks per year.

	Bricklayers	Labourers
Working hours week	40	40
Normal idle time	15%	15%
Holidays per year	4 wks full pay	4 wks full pay
Wage rate per hour	£6	£4
Weekly bonus (paid only for working weeks)	£40	£20
Lodging allowance (wk)	£100	£85
Non-contributory pension fund – employer's payment per year	£615	–
No. of Employees	3	2

G. & H. Clothing Manufacturers

Background information

G. & H. Clothing Manufacturers make shirts and blouses for some of the large retail stores. Recently demand for their clothing has increased due to the high quality of goods produced. The owner of the business Larry Ahmed has decided he would like more information on his labour costs to enable more accurate costings to be made. He supplies you with the following information:

Operation	Time per operation (minutes)	Employee grade	Wages per hour £
Cutting	10 mins	1	3.50
Sewing	20 mins	2	3.85
Accessories	15 mins	3	4.20
Pressing	8 mins	4	3.50
Packaging	10 mins	5	3.00

At the moment all employees work 36 hours a week and a production target of 600 dozen items has been set.

▶**Task**

You are required to calculate the following:

(i) Total number of workers required

(ii) Weekly cost of each operation

(iii) The total labour cost for a week

Round figures off to the nearest whole number.

SIMULATION 40

Milligan & Bagshaw

Background information

Milligan & Bagshaw operate a manufacturing business which has three staff, Ernie, Ken and Ron. Their remuneration details are shown below.

	Ernie	Ken	Ron
Rate per hour	£3.90	£3.60	£4.20
Rate per unit	£0.70	£0.30	£0.65
Units produced	240	350	250
Time allowed in minutes per unit	12	5	10
Time taken in hours	40	25	35

▶**Task**

You are required to calculate the remuneration of each employee using the following methods:

(i) The hourly rate

(ii) Basic piece rate

(iii) Bonus scheme based on time saved.

Welch & Partners

Unit 6
Recording Cost Information
Element 6.2
Operate and maintain a system of accounting for labour costs
Performance criteria **a b c d**

Background information

Welch & Partners are a small engineering company which employs three people. The following information relates to the employees and units produced for one week:

Employee	John Seymour	Richard Mayall	Ian Chapman
No. of units produced	90	75	66
Time allowed per unit (minutes)	30	32	40
Time taken in hours	38	36	40
Rate per hour	£5.00	£4.75	£5.20
Rate per unit	£2.25	£2.45	£3.35

▶ **Task 1**

You are required to calculate the remuneration of each employee using the following methods:

(i) Hourly rate

(ii) Basic piece rate

(iii) Individual bonus scheme, where each worker receives a bonus in proportion to the time saved by the time allowed.

▶ **Task 2**

What advantages are there to both the employer and employee in using Method (iii) – Individual Bonus Scheme.

MA & F

Cost Accountant

Unit 6
Recording Cost Information
Element 6.2
Operate and maintain a system of accounting for labour costs
Performance criteria **a b c d e**

Background information

How would a Cost Accountant account for the following in ascertaining total costs?

(i) overtime premium;
(ii) incentive payment;
(iii) sick pay and holiday pay to operatives;
(iv) idle time.

An organisation operates an individual premium bonus scheme in which an operative's performance is calculated and paid for as follows: Each task is given a target expressed in standard minutes. The amount of weekly output achieved is stated as a total of standard minutes. The week's total of standard minutes is expressed as a percentage of attendance time (to the nearest whole number). The operator is paid:

Percentage Performance	Rate Paid Per Hour
0–75	£2.20
76–90	£2.40
91–110	£2.80
111 and over	£3.40

Three products are assembled and have the following standard times:

Product A – 42 standard minutes
Product B – 60 standard minutes
Product C – 75 standard minutes

▶**Task**

Calculate the gross pay for each operator from the following information:

Operator	Hours Attended	Performance Products Assembled		
		A	B	C
Smith	38	15	13	11
Jones	39	15	10	8
Brown	42	15	18	16

Association of Accounting Technicians

Ainsworth & Co.

Background information

Ainsworth & Co. are situated in Devon and produce one single product, sun umbrellas which are sold both in the UK and overseas. The company employs ten staff who are directly involved in production, they work 36 hours a week and are paid £5.00 per hour, with a guaranteed wage of £180 per week. Any overtime worked is at time and a half with a maximum of 15 hours overtime allowed per week per employee. Due to unforeseen circumstances additional labour cannot be recruited.

The average time to produce one umbrella is 40 mins and at present the company produces 300 per week. However, as the summer season gets under way demand is well in excess of the company's production capacity, in spite of working overtime.

The company manager, Mike Chapman, decides to hold a management meeting with a view to introducing a wage incentive scheme. The outcome of the meeting is an increase in the hourly wage rate to £5.50 per hour, if the standard time to produce one unit is reduced to 35 mins. Overtime would still be paid at time and a half with the minimum guaranteed wage rising to £198 per week.

In addition to the labour cost, materials cost £10 per unit and the umbrellas sell for £25 each.

▶Task

You are required to calculate the total profit and profit per unit if demand for the umbrellas for one week is as follows:

(i) 450 umbrellas
(ii) 600 umbrellas
(iii) 750 umbrellas

(a) If the present wages scheme is maintained, and
(b) If the new incentive scheme is introduced.

Overhead costs should be ignored and you should round your figures to the nearest pound.

(c) Comment on your findings.

Earnings calculations

Background information

Below are details of a company's records relating to labour costs:

(a) Normal working day: 8 hours
Guaranteed rate of pay (on time basis) £5.5 per hour
Standard time allowed to produce
1 unit: 3 minutes
Piecework price: £0.1 per standard minute
Premium Bonus 75% of time saved, in addition to hourly pay.

(b) Assume that in a budget period of 4 weeks (5 working days per week), the actual data for the performance of one man is as follows:

Actual hours paid: 160 hours
Actual hours worked: 140 hours
Actual units produced: 2,700 units
Actual wages paid: £1,000

▶**Task 1**

For the following levels of output produced in one day:

80 units
120 units
210 units

Calculate earnings based on:

(i) piecework, where earnings are guaranteed at 80% of time based pay
(ii) premium bonus system.

▶**Task 2**

Using the standard date in (a) above, calculate the total wages variance, with sub-analysis of the variance as you think appropriate. You should assume that remuneration is based on a time basis.

Association of Accounting Technicians

Moores & Sons Ltd

Background information

Moores & Sons Ltd are a small family business who occupy two units on a local industrial estate for the manufacture of office furniture and fittings. The following is a list of the company's expenses.

▶**Task**

You are required to allocate these expenses under the appropriate headings:

Work-in-Progress Control A/c.
Factory Overheads A/c.
Fixed Plant & Machinery A/c.
Selling & Distribution Overhead A/c.
Administration Overhead A/c.

Moores & Sons Ltd – Company Expenses

Rent of factory
Heating and Lighting
    – Factory
    – Offices

Insurance
    – Plant and machinery
    – Office equipment

Advertising
Marketing manager's salary
Printing and stationery
    – Office
    – Promotional material

Supervisors' wages
    – Production
Direct labour
Direct material
Carriage outwards
Office salaries and wages
Repairs and maintenance
    – Plant and machinery
    – Office equipment

Direct expenses
    – Royalties
Depreciation
    – Plant and machinery
    – Office equipment

Salesman's commission and salary
New circular saw

MA & F

SIMULATION 46

Unit 6
Recording Cost Information
Element 6.3
Operate and maintain a system of accounting for expenses Performance criteria **a c**

Newton's Manufacturing Co.

Background information

Newton's Manufacturing Co. produces goods for the motor car industry. During a recent financial period the company incurred the following items of expenditure:

(i)   Cost of installing new plant and machinery.
(ii)   Payment of directors' salaries
(iii)   Payment of debenture interest
(iv)   Purchase of materials used in production
(v)   Direct labour
(vi)   Maintenance charges on office equipment
(vii)   Purchase of new plant and equipment
(viii) Cost of improvements to factory heating system
(ix)   Salary of salesman
(x)   Cleaning expenses – Factory.

▶ **Task 1**

You are required to give a definition of each of the following terms:

(i)   Revenue Expenditure
(ii)   Capital Expenditure.

▶ **Task 2**

Construct a table which shows, for each of the items (i) to (x), whether the item should be regarded as revenue or capital expenditure.

▶ **Task 3**

The company uses an 'Integral Accounts System' which provides both financial and management accounting information. Using the following headings, allocate each of the items (i) to (x):

Work-in-Progress Control A/c.
Factory Overheads A/c.
Fixed Plant and Equipment A/c.
Fixed Buildings A/c.
Selling and Distribution Overhead A/c.
Administration Overhead A/c.

Rowland Timber Products Ltd

Unit 6
Recording Cost Information
Element 6.3
Operate and maintain a system of accounting for expenses Performance criteria **a b c**

Background information

Rowland Timber Products are situated in Ipswich and are manufacturers of doors and window frames for direct supply to building contractors or builders' merchants. The company operates within three departments and Job No. ZS 23 was carried out in all three. Details of the job were as follows:

Department	Direct materials £	Direct wages £	Direct labour hours
A	1,950	2,400	500
B	2,820	900	400
C	690	1,995	600

Works overhead is recovered on the basis of direct labour hours and administrative overhead as a percentage of works cost.

The figures for the last period for the three departments, on which the current overhead recovery rates are based, were:

Departments	A	B	C
Direct material	£18,375	£34,080	£77,340
Direct wages	£28,125	£70,200	£163,200
Direct labour hours	6,000	8,000	9,000
Works overhead	£15,000	£21,600	£28,800
Administrative overhead	£8,610	£44,058	£26,934

The company's profit margin is 30%.

▶Task

You are required to draw up a Cost Ledger Sheet showing the cost of Job ZS 23 and the price charged to the customer.

MA & F

SIMULATION 48

Unit 6
Recording Cost Information
Element 6.3
Operate and maintain a system of accounting for expenses Performance criteria **a b c**

Overheads

A manufacturing concern absorbs overheads by means of budgeted departmental rates which are as follows:

PRODUCTION DEPARTMENTS	ABSORPTION
Machine Shop	£1.20 per machine hour worked
Finishing Shop	80% on direct wages
Assembly	£0.25 per unit of finished product
NON-PRODUCTIVE DEPARTMENTS	125% on direct material cost, issued to Production

For the previous period the following was incurred:

	Direct Materials Issued £	Direct Wages Earned £	Machine Hours Worked	Actual Overhead £
Machine Shop	4,160	6,650	9,600	11,570
Finishing Shop	23,520	12,700	–	9,470
Assembly	11,020	3,700		15,110
Non-Productive Depts				49,135
	£38,700	£23,050		£85,285

During the period 58,500 units were manufactured.

▶Task 1

Calculate for each department and in total:

(i)   the amount of overhead absorbed into total costs
(ii) the amount of under or over absorbed overhead.

▶Task 2

Calculate the amount of profit or loss made by Job Number 872 which was completed during the period from the following information:

Selling Price £3 unit. Quantity 1,152 units.

	Material £	Wages £	Machine hours
Machine Shop	150	101	315
Finishing Shop	470	200	
Assembly	160	74	

▶Task 3

State an alternative method of recovering overheads which the company could use, indicating whether this would be an improvement on the existing method.

Association of Accounting Technicians

MA & F

Bellmont Co. Ltd

Background information

The Bellmont Co. Ltd has three production departments, drilling, turning and finishing. The following information relates to the drilling department for a cost period:

	Drilling Department		Actual Data for
	Budgeted Data	Actual Data	Job No. D201
Direct material	£100,000	£140,000	£6,000
Direct labour	£200,000	£250,000	£3,000
Production overhead	£200,000	£230,000	
Direct labour hours	50,000	62,500	750
Machine hours	40,000	50,000	750

▶**Task 1**

Calculate the production overhead absorption rate predetermined for the period based upon:

(i)   percentage of direct material cost and
(ii) machine hours.

▶**Task 2**

Calculate the production overhead to be charged to Job D201 based on the rate calculated in answer to (i) above.

▶**Task 3**

Compare your answer to Task 2 assuming that a machine hour absorption rate was in use and calculate the over/under absorption of production overheads for the period and state the appropriate treatment in the accounts.

▶**Task 4**

(i)   Prepare the job cost statements for each method and
(ii) Comment on the relative merits of the two methods of absorption.

MA & F

SIMULATION 50

Manufacturing Department

The following data relates to a manufacturing department for a period:

	Budget £	Actual Data £
Direct material cost	100,000	150,000
Direct labour cost	250,000	275,000
Production overhead	250,000	350,000
Direct labour hours	50,000 hours	55,000 hours

Job ZX was one of the jobs worked on during the period. Direct material costing £7,000 and direct labour (800 hours) costing £4,000 were incurred.

▶ **Task 1**

Calculate the production overhead absorption rate predetermined for the period based on:

(a) percentage of direct material cost
(b) direct labour hours.

▶ **Task 2**

Calculate the production overhead cost to be charged to Job ZX based on the rates calculated in answer to Task 1.

▶ **Task 3**

Assume that the direct labour hour rate of absorption is used. Calculate the under or over absorption of production overheads for the period and state an appropriate treatment in the accounts.

▶ **Task 4**

Comment briefly on the relative merits of the two methods of overhead absorption used in Task 1.

Association of Accounting Technicians

MA & F

Seddon's Manufacturers

Background information

Seddon's Manufacturers make two products, garden forks and spades. The total budget for overheads in the next year is £59,800. Other budget costs and details are as follows:

	Forks	Spades
Number produced	7,500	4,000
Prime cost –	£	£
Labour		
– 48 mins x £3 per hour	2.40	
– 48 mins x £5 per hour		4.00
Material		
–	3.20	4.00
TOTAL PRIME COST	£5.60	£8.00

▶**Task 1**

Calculate the following overhead recovery rates:

(a) Direct labour hour
(b) Direct Material Percentage Rate
(c) Direct Wages Percentage Rate
(d) Prime Cost Percentage Rate.

▶**Task 2**

For each product i.e. fork and spade, show the overhead and total cost by each of the four overhead methods.

SIMULATION 52^A

C. Lloyd Wood (Mfr) Co.

Unit 6
Recording Cost Information
Element 6.4
Operate and maintain a system for the apportionment and absorption of indirect costs (overheads) Performance criteria **a b c d**

Background information

C. Lloyd Wood is a manufacturing company situated in Ripon, Yorkshire. The company comprises three departments – Depts A, B and C plus one service department. Information relating to these departments is as follows:

	Manufacturing Department			Service Dept
	A	B	C	
Book value of plant & equipment	£35,000	£42,000	£59,500	£38,500
Floor area (sq. metres)	3,500	3,500	5,250	2,625
Volume (cubic metres)	11,025	11,725	15,750	7,875
No. of employees	88	88	112	46

The service department spends the following time in each production department:

Department	A	35%
Department	B	40%
Department	C	25%

The company produces three products, namely, Components 1, 2 and 3. The budgeted figures for the first quarter of 19X3 were as follows:

		£
Depreciation	– factory	2,800
	– equipment	1,575
Insurance costs – equipment		525
Lighting		875
Heating		700
Repairs and renewals – factory		875
Office costs		3,500
		10,850

Plus:

	Manufacturing Departments		
	A	B	C
Direct materials cost	56,000	59,850	78,750
Direct labour cost	49,000	50,400	65,625
Machine hours	2,450	2,450	2,450
Output (units)	3,500	3,150	2,625

▶Task

You are required to calculate the total cost of each unit for each of three departments A, B and C absorbing overheads on:

(i) Unit Output Basis
(ii) Machine-hour Basis

Round figures to the nearest pound/pence.

MA & F

SIMULATION 53^A

AAT Company

Unit 6
Recording Cost Information
Element 6.4
Operate and maintain a system for the apportionment and absorption of indirect costs (overheads) Performance criteria **a b c d**

Background information

The AAT company has two departments A and B engaged in manufacturing operations and they are serviced by a Stores Maintenance Department and Tool Room.

The following has been budgeted for the next financial period:

Overheads (£'000s)

	Total	A	B	Stores	Maintenance	Tool Room
Indirect Labour	1,837	620	846	149	115	107
Supervision	140					
Power	160					
Rent	280					
Rates	112					
Plant insurance	40					
Plant Depreciation	20					
	£2,589					

Additional information available includes:

	A	B	Stores	Maintenance	Tool Room
Floor area (square metres)	1,000	2,500	1,100	600	400
Number of employees	30	50	10	20	30
Power (kilowatt hours)	60,000	30,000	3,000	15,000	12,000
Number of material requisitions	5,000	6,000	–	2,000	3,000
Maintenance hours	8,000	9,000	–	–	6,000
Plant valuation (£)	50,000	40,000	–	5,000	5,000
Tool Room hours estimated	7,000	10,000	–	–	–
Machine hours estimated	55,200	99,000	–	–	–

▶ **Task 1**

You are required to calculate appropriate machine hour overhead absorption rates for both manufacturing departments in which all overheads will be recovered and to show clearly the method of overhead allocation.

▶ **Task 2**

Define:

(i) Conversion cost, and
(ii) Added value and explain the principal difference between the two terms.

Association of Accounting Technicians

SIMULATION 54

Cost Accountant – Industrial Concern

Unit 6
Recording Cost Information
Element 6.4
Operate and maintain a system for the apportionment and absorption of indirect costs (overheads) Performance criteria **a b c d**

Background information

You are the Cost Accountant of an industrial concern and have been given the following budgeted information regarding the four cost centres within your organisation.

	Department 1 £	Department 2 £	Maintenance Department £	Canteen £	Total £
Indirect labour	60,000	70,000	25,000	15,000	170,000
Consumables	12,000	16,000	3,000	10,000	41,000
Heating & lighting					12,000
Rent & rates					18,000
Depreciation					30,000
Supervision					24,000
Power					20,000
					315,000

You are also given the following information:

	Department 1	Department 2	Maintenance Department	Canteen	Total
Floor space in square metres	10,000	12,000	5,000	3,000	30,000
Book value of machinery in £	150,000	120,000	20,000	10,000	300,000
Number of employees	40	30	10		80
Kilowatt hours	4,500	4,000	1,000	500	10,000

You are also told:

(i)   The canteen staff are outside contractors.
(ii) Departments 1 and 2 are production cost centres and the maintenance department and canteen are service cost centres.
(iii) The maintenance department provides 4,000 service hours to Department 1 and 3,000 service hours to Department 2.
(iv) That Department 1 is machine intensive and Department 2 is labour intensive.
(v)   That 6,320 machine hours and 7,850 labour hours are budgeted for Departments 1 and 2 respectively for 19X1.

▶ Task 1

An overhead cost statement showing the allocation and apportionment of overhead to the four cost centres for 19X1, clearly showing the basis of apportionment is required.

MA & F

▶Task 2

Calculate the overhead absorption rates for Department 1 on the basis of the machine hours and Department 2 on the basis of labour hours.

▶Task 3

On the basis that for 19X1 actual overheads for Department 1 turn out to be £155,000 and machine hours worked 6,000, whilst actual overheads for Department 2 turn out to be £156,000 and labour hours worked 7,900, calculate the under or over recovery of overheads for each department.

▶Task 4

The Managing Director of your organisation suggests to you that one blanket rate rather than separate overhead absorption rates for Department 1 and 2 based on machine hours and labour hours respectively would be more beneficial for future years.

Draft a reply to this assertion.

Association of Accounting Technicians

SIMULATION 55^A

Simple Ltd

Background information

The Simple company has two production departments and one service department that carries out maintenance work.

The overhead absorption rates used for the month of November were based on:

	Machining	Finishing
Estimated overhead	£15,510	£6,400
Estimated machine hours	2,350	
Estimated direct labour hours		1,280

The above cost estimates include an amount for maintenance department costs that have been apportioned on the basis of total expenses for each production department.

For the month of November, the following costs were incurred:

	Machining	Finishing	Maintenance
Indirect material	2,900	1,600	1,750
Indirect labour	1,620	450	2,400
Depreciation	1,500	250	1,900
Lighting & heating	400	250	150
Supervision	1,420	710	980
Rent & rates	800	500	300
Insurances	1,200	200	1,600
Actual direct labour hours		1,320	
Actual machine hours	2,490		

▶ **Task 1**

Calculate the overhead absorption rates in use during November.

▶ **Task 2**

Prepare a statement showing the overhead costs charged to each production department for November.

▶ **Task 3**

Calculate the amount of under- and over-absorbed overhead for each production department.

MA & F

▶Task 4

Analyse the under- or over-absorbed overhead into the variances that may have caused this feature.

▶Task 5

Discuss the general principles involved in allocating or apportioning overhead to departments or cost centres.

▶Task 6

Show the accounting entries for each of the two production departments assuming the costing system requires any under- or over-absorbed overhead to be calculated at each month end.

Association of Accounting Technicians

Manufacturing Company

Background information

A manufacturing company has prepared the following budgeted information for 19X2:

	£
Direct material	800,000
Direct labour	200,000
Direct expenses	40,000
Production overhead	600,000
Administrative overhead	328,000

Budgeted activity levels include:

Budgeted production	600,000 units
Machine hours	50,000
Labour hours	40,000

It has recently spent heavily upon advanced technological machinery and reduced its workforce. As a consequence it is thinking about changing its basis for overhead absorption from a percentage of direct labour cost to either a machine hour or labour hour basis. The administrative overhead is to be absorbed as a percentage of factory cost.

▶**Task 1**

Prepare pre-determined overhead absorption rates for production overhead based upon the three different bases for absorption mentioned above.

▶**Task 2**

Outline the reasons for calculating a pre-determined overhead absorption rate.

▶**Task 3**

Select the overhead absorption rate that you think the organisation should use giving reasons for your decision.

▶**Task 4**

The company has been asked to price job AX, this job requires the following:

Direct material	£3,788
Direct labour	£1,100
Direct expenses	£422
Machine hours	120
Labour hours	220

Compute the price for this job using the absorption rate selected in Task 3 above, given that the company profit margin is equal to 10% of the price.

▶**Task 5**

The company previously paid its direct labour workers upon a time basis but is now contemplating moving over to an incentive scheme.

Draft a memo to the Chief Accountant outlining the general characteristics and advantages of employing a successful incentive scheme.

Association of Accounting Technicians

SIMULATION 57^A

RST Company

Unit 6
Recording Cost Information
Element 6.4
Operate and maintain a system for the apportionment and absorption of indirect costs (overheads) Performance criteria **a b c d**

Background information

The management of RST Company realise that additional marketing/ distribution cost studies are needed, but the company lacks the personnel and funds at present to establish accurate cost standards. They do believe, however, that they may be accepting orders that are too small. As a result, they analysed the order sizes received last year and have broken down their orders into the simple categories of small (1–20 items), medium (21–100 items) and large (over 100 items).

The actual marketing and distribution costs incurred last year were as follows:

Cost	Amount (£)	Basis for apportionment
Marketing personnel salaries	27,000	Number of personnel
Marketing manager's salary	20,000	Time spent
Sales people's commissions	3,000	Amount of sales
Advertising and direct selling	37,500	Amount of sales
Packing and shipping	26,250	Weight shipped
Delivery	19,000	Weight shipped
Credit and collect	15,000	Number of orders

An analysis of their records had produced the following statistics:

	Order sizes			
	Small	Medium	Large	Total
Number of personnel	5	3	1	9
Time spent by marketing manager	60%	10%	30%	100%
Amount of sales (£)	250,000	300,000	200,000	750,000
Weight	6,090	2,940	1,470	10,500
Number of orders	612	170	68	850

▶**Task 1**

Prepare a detailed schedule showing the full marketing cost per order size and marketing cost as a percentage of total sales for each order size.

▶**Task 2**

What recommendations would you make to management regarding the size of order they should accept?

Chartered Institute of Marketing

MA & F

Preparing VAT Returns

Standards of Competence

ELEMENT 8.1 PREPARE VAT RETURNS

Performance Criteria

a VAT returns are correctly completed from the appropriate sources and submitted within the statutory time limits

b Relevant inputs and outputs are correctly identified and calculated

c VAT documentation is correctly filed

d Submissions are made in accordance with currently operative VAT laws and regulations

e Discussions with VAT inspectors are conducted openly and constructively to promote the efficiency of the VAT accounting system

Range Statement

- Exempt supplies, zero rated supplies, imports and exports

Knowledge and Understanding

The business environment
- Basic law and practice relating to all issues covered in the range statement and referred to in the performance criteria. Specific issues include:
  - the classification of types of supply
  - registration requirements
  - the form of VAT invoices; tax points
- Sources of information on VAT: Customs and Excise Guide
- Administration of VAT; enforcement

The organisation

Background understanding that the accounting systems of an organisation are affected by its organisational structure; its administrative systems and procedures and the nature of its business transactions

Background understanding that recording and accounting practices may vary in different parts of the organisation

Louise

Background information

Louise has been working as a trainee accountant for a local sports manufacturer but owing to cutbacks within the company was recently made redundant. Fortunately, the company was able to offer her part-time work consisting of ten hours a week. Louise had always had an ambition to work for herself so decides that this is the ideal opportunity. In addition to the part-time work with her former employer she has steadily been increasing the number of clients to whom she offers book-keeping and secretarial services, plus the preparation and completion of VAT Returns.

Many of Louise's clients are in similar circumstances to herself, starting their own small business. One of the areas that she is frequently being asked questions about is the VAT procedure.

Louise decides that she could do with a simple guide to VAT procedures, when the following questions could be addressed.

▶Task

Individually, or in a small group, produce a pamphlet 'Simple Guide to VAT Procedures', using the following headings, ideally this should be carried out using a word-processor.

(1) Legal background – including the initial introduction of VAT

(2) VAT rates

(3) Classification of goods –
    Standard rate supplies
    Zero rated supplies
    Exempt supplies

(4) Zero rated goods and services
    Examples

(5) Exempted goods and services
    Examples

(6) Taxable persons
    Examples

(7) Mandatory registration

(8) Voluntary registration

(9) Account and records:
    – Tax invoice
    – Tax period
    – How often must a claim be sent?
    – When must the return be submitted?
    – To whom must the return be sent?
    – What records and books do I need to keep and for how long?

(10) Administration
    – Name of Government Department responsible

(11) Completion of VAT Return

(12) How to deal with errors that may have been made on VAT Return

(13) Special areas:
Imports
Exports
Partial exemption
Goods for own use
Bad debts
Purchase of cars

KES 2000

Background information

Mr Tom Akhtar and his son Jamil, run a small clothing manufacturers under the name of 'KES 2000'. They make gents' and ladies' trousers for sale both at home and overseas to EC countries.

At the end of the quarter, 30th June 19X3, Jamil, who is responsible for the accounting functions of the business produces the following information:

'KES 2000'
Period 1st April –30th June 19X3

		£	£
1.	Sales (excluding VAT)		
	UK	150,000	
	France & Germany	30,000	180,000
2.	VAT charged on sales		
	UK (17½% of £150,000)	26,250	
	France & Germany	–	26,250
3.	Purchases (excluding VAT)		
	UK	60,000	
	EC countries	3,000	63,000
4.	VAT charged on purchases		
	UK (17½% of £60,000)	10,500	
	EC countries (17½% of £3,000)	525	11,025

▶**Task**

From the information supplied above, calculate the amount of VAT payable and complete the VAT Form 'VAT 100'.

BASIC INFORMATION TO BE ENTERED ON FORM VAT 100

Before you fill in this form **please read the notes on the back and the VAT Leaflet** *"Filling in your VAT return"*. Complete all boxes clearly in ink, writing 'none' where necessary. Don't put a dash or leave any box blank. If there are no pence write "00" in the pence column. Do not enter more than one amount in any box.

		£	p
For official use	VAT due in this period on **sales** and other outputs	1		
	VAT reclaimed in this period on **purchases** and other inputs	2		
	Net VAT to be paid to Customs or reclaimed by you **(Difference between boxes 1 and 2)**	3		
	Total value of **sales** and all other outputs excluding any VAT. **Include your box 6 figure**	4		00
	Total value of **purchases** and all other inputs excluding any VAT. **Include your box 7 figure**	5		00
	Total value of all **sales** and related services to other **EC Member States**	6		00
	Total value of all **purchases** and related services from other **EC Member States**	7		00

Retail schemes. If you have used any of the schemes in the period covered by this return please enter the appropriate letter(s) in this box.

If you are enclosing a payment please tick this box.

DECLARATION by the signatory to be completed by or on behalf of the person named above.

I,..declare that the

(Full name of signatory in BLOCK LETTERS)

information given above is true and complete.

Signature ....Date .... 19 ....

A false declaration can result in prosecution.

VAT 100   CD 2850/N9(02/91)   F 3790 (January 1992)

© Crown Copyright

Chapman Pressing Co.

Unit 8
Preparing VAT Returns
Element 8.1
Prepare VAT returns Performance criteria **a b c d**

Background information

Chapman Pressings is a small company which manufactures exhaust clips used in the motor car industry. The company sells mainly to the UK market but recently has been supplying the product to EC countries. His wife, Carol, keeps the books of account and for the quarter ended 30th November 19X2 supplies the following information:

Period 1st September – 30th November 19X2

		£	£
1.	Sales (excluding VAT)		
	– UK	75,000	
	– EC countries	56,000	131,000
2.	Output tax on sales		
	– UK	13,125	
	– EC countries	NIL	13,125
3.	Purchases (excluding VAT)		
	– UK	70,600	
	– EC countries	1,600	72,100
4.	VAT charged on purchases		
	– UK	12,355	
	– EC countries	280	12,635

▶**Task 1**

From the information supplied, calculate the amount of VAT payable.

▶**Task 2**

Complete VAT 100 Form.

▶**Task 3**

State when the VAT Form should be sent to Customs and Excise.

▶**Task 4**

One of the company's customers has become insolvent owing a total of £300 (including VAT), the debt has been outstanding for over a year. Advise the company on this matter.

BASIC INFORMATION TO BE ENTERED ON FORM VAT 100

Before you fill in this form **please read the notes on the back and the VAT Leaflet** *"Filling in your VAT return"*. Complete all boxes clearly in ink, writing 'none' where necessary. Don't put a dash or leave any box blank. If there are no pence write "00" in the pence column. Do not enter more than one amount in any box.

		£	p
For official use	VAT due in this period on **sales** and other outputs	1	
	VAT reclaimed in this period on **purchases** and other inputs	2	
	Net VAT to be paid to Customs or reclaimed by you **(Difference between boxes 1 and 2)**	3	
	Total value of **sales** and all other outputs excluding any VAT. **Include your box 6 figure**	4	00
	Total value of **purchases** and all other inputs excluding any VAT. **Include your box 7 figure**	5	00
	Total value of all **sales** and related services to other **EC Member States**	6	00
	Total value of all **purchases** and related services from other **EC Member States**	7	00

Retail schemes. If you have used any of the schemes in the period covered by this return please enter the appropriate letter(s) in this box.

If you are enclosing a payment please tick this box.

DECLARATION by the signatory to be completed by or on behalf of the person named above.

I,..declare that the

(Full name of signatory in BLOCK LETTERS)

information given above is true and complete.

Signature ....Date .... 19 ....

A false declaration can result in prosecution.

VAT 100   CD 2850/N9(02/91)   F 3790 (January 1992)

Mr Dennis Bayley

	Unit 8
	Preparing VAT Returns
	Element 8.1
	Prepare VAT returns Performance criteria **a b c d**

Background information

Mr Dennis Bayley runs his own small manufacturing company and submits his VAT returns for the quarter ending 31st March, 30th June, 30th September and 31st December.

The following details relate to transactions for the quarter ending 31st March 19X2:

Purchases Invoices				
Tax Point	Invoice No.	Total £	Goods £	VAT £
8.1.X2	100	982.70	836.34	146.36
15.1.X2	101	1,646.96	1,401.67	245.29
30.1.X2	102	3,055.45	2,600.38	455.07
16.2.X2	103	3,397.57	2,891.55	506.02
23.2.X2	104	1,522.22	1,295.51	226.71
1.3.X2	105	210.03	178.75	31.28
16.3.X2	106	1,368.83	1,164.96	203.87
		12,183.76	10,369.16	1,814.60

Sales Invoices				
Tax Point	Invoice No.	Total £	Goods £	VAT £
31.1.X2	0027	5,226.54	4,448.12	778.42
3.2.X2	0028	2,639.56	2,246.43	393.13
28.2.X2	0029	1,709.63	1,455.00	254.63
7.3.X2	0030	3,713.45	3,160.38	553.07
14.3.X2	0031	340.22	289.55	50.67
20.3.X2	0032	4,701.96	4,001.67	700.29
27.3.X2	0033	2,548.75	2,169.15	379.60
		20,880.11	17,770.30	3,109.81

▶**Task 1**

Compute the net VAT payable for the quarter to 31st March 19X2.

▶**Task 2**

Complete the VAT Form for Mr Bayley whose business address is:
Unit 30, West Park Industrial Estate, Bradford, Yorkshire
VAT Registration No. 914 6159 66
Period 1st January 19X2 to 31st March 19X2

BA1 Ch 19

Value Added Tax Return

For the period

to

Registration number

Period

You could be liable to a financial penalty if your completed return and all the VAT payable are not received by the due date.

Due date:

For official use D O R only	

Before you fill in this form **please read the notes on the back and the VAT Leaflet** "*Filling in your VAT return*". Complete all boxes clearly in ink, writing 'none' where necessary. Don't put a dash or leave any box blank. If there are no pence write "00" in the pence column. Do not enter more than one amount in any box.

For official use		£	p
	VAT due in this period on **sales** and other outputs	1	
	VAT reclaimed in this period on **purchases** and other inputs	2	
	Net VAT to be paid to Customs or reclaimed by you **(Difference between boxes 1 and 2)**	3	
	Total value of **sales** and all other outputs excluding any VAT. **Include your box 6 figure**	4	00
	Total value of **purchases** and all other inputs excluding any VAT. **Include your box 7 figure**	5	00
	Total value of all **sales** and related services to other **EC Member States**	6	00
	Total value of all **purchases** and related services from other **EC Member States**	7	00

Retail schemes. If you have used any of the schemes in the period covered by this return please enter the appropriate letter(s) in this box.

If you are enclosing a payment please tick this box.

DECLARATION by the signatory to be completed by or on behalf of the person named above.

I,...declare that the

(Full name of signatory in BLOCK LETTERS)

information given above is true and complete.

Signature ....Date ....19 ....

A false declaration can result in prosecution.

VAT 100   CD 2850/N9(02/91)   F 3790 (January 1992)

© Crown copyright

Hall Supplies

Background information

Hall Supplies is a medium-sized engineering company situated at Stanley Mill, Castle Street, Manchester, MK11 3NW. The firm sells all of its products in the UK and purchases their supplies from local businesses. On the following pages are lists of their purchases and sales invoices for the quarter ended 28th February 19X3. The invoice total includes VAT where appropriate. The following VAT code has been used:

1 – Standard rate
0 – Zero rated items

▶**Task 1**

You are required to calculate the amount of VAT on each invoice, with reference to the VAT code and using a rate of 17½%, and list them using the following headings:

Date	Customer	Invoice number	Total	Goods subject to VAT	Zero rated	VAT

▶**Task 2**

Calculate the amount of VAT due for the quarter.

▶**Task 3**

Complete the VAT 100 Form.

This exercise is intended to be done using a computer spreadsheet but can be done manually.

Hall Supplies
Purchase Invoices
Period 1st December 19X2 to 28th February 19X3

Date			Customer	Invoice Number	Invoice Total (£)	VAT Code
19X2						
Dec	.7		Thompson's	2467	250.00	1
	9		Hughes Bros.	2468	159.83	1
	10		Hacket & Sons	2469	236.00	1
	11		McMurty Bros. Ltd	2470	34.93	0
	12		–,,–	2471	49.35	0
	15		Platt's	2473	60.84	1
	16		Smiths (Supplies) Ltd	2474	295.51	1
	18		Currington (Mfrs) Ltd	2475	259.09	1
	19		Leigh & Allen (Ins.) Co.	2476	472.70	1
	22		A.V. Barlow	2477	836.34	1
	23		Phillips & Associates	2478	145.00	0
	28		Dicksons Ltd	2479	1,455.00	1
	28		Perkins & Phillips	2480	158.62	1
	,,		–,,–	2481	5.40	1
	,,		–,,–	2482	18.68	1
	,,		–,,–	2483	88.31	1
	29		–,,–	2484	289.55	1
	31		Mollets	2485	54.16	0
19X3						
Jan	4		B.M.J. Co.	2486	178.75	1
	,,		British Telecom	2487	109.58	1
	5		S.J. Hughes & Sons	2488	401.67	1
	7		Rowley & Rawlinson	2489	9.00	0
	12		Chesters Timber	2490	57.00	1
	13		Perkins & Phillips	2491	23.90	1
	14		E.J. Electrical	2492	160.38	1
	17		Thos. George Garage	2493	95.29	1
	23		Hacket & Sons	2494	35.17	1
	,,		–,,–	2495	72.50	1
	,,		–,,–	2496	38.10	1
	24		Hughes Bros.	2497	18.68	1
	26		McMurty Bros Ltd	2498	164.96	0
	27		Smiths (Supplies) Ltd	2499	180.97	1
	30		Hoye & Glicher	2500	174.38	1
	31		Rogers & Rowlands	2501	33.17	0
	,,		–,,–	2502	72.18	0
	,,		–,,–	2503	289.55	1
Feb	1		Alpha & Son	2504	258.03	1
	3		Fleming Thorn plc	2505	1,104.00	1
	4		Beacon	2506	692.21	1
	10		B.M.J. Co	2507	855.33	1
	13		Perry & Sutton	2508	681.32	1
	17		Britt Partners	2509	153.07	1
	23		Harris's	2510	48.18	0
	24		–,,–	2511	169.91	0
	27		Richardson Co.	2512	47.00	0
	,,		A.V. Barlow	2513	107.50	1
	28		Hoye & Glicher	2514	259.09	1
	,,		Clark's	2515	160.38	1

Date		Customer	Invoice Number	Invoice Total (£)	VAT Code
19X2					
Dec	1	Isherwoods Supplies Ltd	S.5010	31.32	1
	8	Bolton Products	S.5011	568.61	1
	10	Pickford & Partners	S.5012	200.00	1
	,,	Crawford Mfr.	S.5013	2,941.51	1
	12	Oldfield & Twigg	S.5014	448.36	1
	15	D.M. Electrical Contractors	S.5015	2,169.15	1
	22	Webb & Stewart	S.5016	1,140.00	1
	28	Badger Promotions	S.5017	692.21	1
	30	Isherwoods Supplies Ltd	S.5018	4,855.67	1
19X3					
Jan	3	Davis, Brown & Associates	S.5019	1,153.07	1
	7	Webb & Stewart	S.5020	3,992.50	1
	17	G R (Manufacturing) Co.	S.5021	1,187.00	1
	23	Wain Bros.	S.5022	340.49	1
	24	Crawford Mfr.	S.5023	1,204.80	1
	27	D.M. Electrical Contractors	S.5024	500.00	1
	30	Beacon plc	S.5025	331.66	1
	31	Bolton Products	S.5026	57.60	1
Feb	1	Webb & Stewart	S.5027	2,553.23	1
	8	Unsworth & Son	S.5028	262.79	1
	10	Howard Supplies & Co.	S.5029	1,027.00	1
	12	Pickford & Partners	S.5030	2,169.15	1
	14	Duffield & Hall	S.5031	723.52	1
	16	Massey & Sons	S.5032	964.24	1
	23	Cameron Bros.	S.5033	141.97	1
	28	Dale & Sons	S.5034	195.05	1
	,,	Wain Bros.	S.5035	3,092.43	1

Before you fill in this form **please read the notes on the back and the VAT Leaflet** "*Filling in your VAT return*". Complete all boxes clearly in ink, writing 'none' where necessary. Don't put a dash or leave any box blank. If there are no pence write "00" in the pence column. Do not enter more than one amount in any box.

		£	p
For official use	VAT due in this period on **sales** and other outputs	1	
	VAT reclaimed in this period on **purchases** and other inputs	2	
	Net VAT to be paid to Customs or reclaimed by you **(Difference between boxes 1 and 2)**	3	
	Total value of **sales** and all other outputs excluding any VAT. **Include your box 6 figure**	4	00
	Total value of **purchases** and all other inputs excluding any VAT. **Include your box 7 figure**	5	00
	Total value of all **sales** and related services to other **EC Member States**	6	00
	Total value of all **purchases** and related services from other **EC Member States**	7	00

Retail schemes. If you have used any of the schemes in the period covered by this return please enter the appropriate letter(s) in this box.

If you are enclosing a payment please tick this box.

DECLARATION by the signatory to be completed by or on behalf of the person named above.

I,..declare that the

(Full name of signatory in BLOCK LETTERS)

information given above is true and complete.

Signature ....Date .... 19 ....

A false declaration can result in prosecution.

VAT 100   CD 2850/N9(02/91)   F 3790 (January 1992)

© Crown Copyright

Brackley (Suppliers' Merchants) Ltd

Background information

Brackley (Suppliers' Merchants) Ltd situated in Manchester, supply goods to the retail trade. The following details relate to the quarter ended 28th February 19X3.

	£
Sales standard rated (excluding VAT)	110,800
Zero rated	17,500
Exempt	32,660
Input tax (VAT only)	
Attributable to taxable supplies	11,080
–"– exempt supplies	1,083
–"– overheads	2,920
Apportionment of overhead expenditure	
Standard rate supplies	60%
Zero rated supplies	20%
Exempt supplies	20%
	100%

▶**Task**

Calculate the VAT payable for the quarter ended 28th February 19X3.

SIMULATION 64

Mrs Lammle

Background information

Mrs Lammle has traded successfully as a shoe designer and manufacturer since 1 January 19X3. She is registered for value added tax (VAT) and all her sales are taxable either at the standard or zero rate.

For the three months to 31 May 19X1, you have extracted the following figures from the accounting records:

	£
Sales:	
To UK customers	30,000
To overseas customers	8,000
Materials:	
Standard rated	4,000
Zero rated	2,000
Exempt	800
Expenses:	
General, all standard rated	6,000
Wages	7,000
Hire of machinery	600
Bank charges, in respect of business bank overdraft	500
Entertaining overseas customers	400

All the above include VAT, if appropriate
Use VAT rate of 17½%.

▶**Task**

Calculate the VAT due in respect of the quarter to 31st May 19X1.

Association of Accounting Technicians (Amended)

Wakem & Co. Ltd

Unit 8
Preparing VAT Returns
Element 8.1
Prepare VAT returns Performance criteria **b d e**

Background information

You have received a letter from the managing director of Wakem & Co. Ltd, a company making wholly standard rated supplies. Extracts from it are as follows:

> During the course of the last quarter sales have been very good. In particular we sold £30,000 worth of goods to St. Oggs Inc an American company and we also sold £20,000 worth to Rappit Ltd in Scotland. Mr Jakin the managing director of Rappit Ltd drove a hard bargain, however, and to secure the order we had to allow a 5% discount for prompt settlement. As we closed down the box manufacturing line, we sold off the machinery and made a useful £15,000. The electrical equipment remaining has been hired to Mudport Ltd for £1,000 a month. One piece of bad news is that Garum Furs plc has gone into liquidation owing us £14,000 though there is the possibility of recovering part of that in the liquidation.

▶**Task 1**

Explain the significance for Value Added Tax of the events described in the letter.

▶**Task 2**

Explain the Value Added Tax significance to a UK trader of making:

(a) wholly standard rated supplies
(b) wholly zero rated supplies
(c) wholly exempt supplies.

Association of Accounting Technicians

BA1 Ch 19

Part 3

SUGGESTED ANSWERS

▶ **Task 1**   *Clothing Manufacturing Business*

(a)	Capital	(f)	Capital
(b)	Revenue	(g)	Capital
(c)	Revenue	(h)	Revenue
(d)	Revenue	(i)	Revenue
(e)	Revenue	(j)	Capital

▶ **Task 2**   *Morgans' Garage*

(a)	Revenue	(f)	Capital
(b)	Capital	(g)	Revenue
(c)	Capital	(h)	Capital
(d)	Revenue	(i)	Revenue
(e)	Revenue	(j)	Revenue

▶ **Task 3**   *Penhalls Advertising and Marketing Co.*

(a)	Revenue	(f)	Revenue
(b)	Capital	(g)	Revenue
(c)	Revenue	(h)	Revenue
(d)	Revenue	(i)	Capital
(e)	Capital	(j)	Capital

SIMULATION 3^A   Laser Printer Depreciation

▶ **Task 1**   *Annual depreciation charges:*

		Annual Depreciation Charge		
	Estimated annual usage Sheets	*Straight Line Method £*	*Diminishing Balance Method £*	*Units of Output £*
Year 1	35,000	450	1,080	350
Year 2	45,000	450	432	450
Year 3	45,000	450	173	450
Year 4	55,000	450	115	550
	180,000	1,800	1,800	1,800

▶Task 2

Laser Printer A/c

19X4		£	19X4		£
Jan1	Balance b/f	1,800	Jul 1	Assets disposals	1,800

Provision for Depreciation—Laser Printer A/c

19X4		£	19X4		£
Jul 1	Assets disposals	1,742	Jan 1	Balance b/f	1,685
			Jul 1	Depreciation	57
		1,742			1,742

Assets Disposals A/c

19X4		£	19X4		£
Jul 1	Laser Printer	1,800	Jul 1	Provision for Depreciation	1,742
Dec 31	Profit and Loss	142	Jul 1	Bank	200
		1,942			1,942

SIMULATION 5^A   John Peacock

▶Task

Workings

i)
		£
1 April 19X8	– Cost of second-hand lorry	40,000
1 May 19X8	– Roadworthy Repairs	5,000

$$\left\{ \begin{array}{l} \text{Total Cost} \\ \text{Capital Expenditure} \end{array} \right. = \underline{\underline{£45,000}}$$

ii) Insurance Premium = £1,200 per year = Revenue expenditure

∴ 7 months = $\dfrac{£1,200 \times 7}{12}$ = £700

iii) *Depreciation*

Straight-line basis with expected life of 5 years

= $\dfrac{£45,000}{5 \text{ yrs}}$ = £9,000 Depreciation per year.

∴ 6 months = £4,500

Dr		Motor Lorry A/c			Cr
19X8			19X8		
1st April	Bank	40,000	31 Oct	Balance c/d	45,000
1st May	Bank				
	(Roadworthy Repairs)	5,000			
		45,000			45,000
1st Nov	Balance b/d	45,000			

Dr		Motor Lorry Provision for Depreciation A/c		Cr
		19X8		
		31st Oct	Profit & Loss A/c (Dep'n 6 mths)	4,500

Dr			Motor Lorry Insurance A/c		Cr
19X8			19X8		
1st April	Bank	1,200	31st Oct	Profit & Loss A/c (Insurance 7 months)	700
			"	Balance c/d	500
		1,200			1,200
1st Nov	Balance b/d	500			

N.B. The cost of repairing the vehicle on 1st July 19X8 as a result of the slight accident would be charged to Motor Expenses A/c.

▶Task 1

Accumulated Fund as at 1st June 19X2

Assets	£
Stocks of food	150
Cash in hand	820
	970
Less Liabilities	
Creditor for food	72
ACCUMULATED FUND	£898

▶Task 2

Cash in hand on 31st May 19X3

Dr		Cash Book		Cr
Balance b/d	820	Payments to suppliers	700	
Subscriptions	3,480	Rent and rates	1,500	
Coffee morning	142	Cleaners' wages	1,900	
Jumble sales	421	Cleaners' materials	152	
Sale of food	880	Treasurer's expenses	275	
Dance proceeds	1,179	Secretarial expenses	345	
		Hi-fi system	1,220	
		Balance c/d	830	
	6,922		6,922	
Balance b/d	830			

Workings

	£
Stock of food	150
Stock of food paid	700
	850
Less creditors 1.6.X2	72
	778
Add creditors 31.5.X3	80
Cost of food used	858

▶Task 3

*Income and Expenditure Account
of Waterfall Social Club yr ended 31.5.X3*

Expenditure	£	Income	£
Rent and rates	1,500	Subscriptions	3,480
Cleaners' wages	1,900	Proceeds of:	
Cleaners' materials	152	Coffee morning	142
Treasurer's expenses	275	Jumble sales	421
Secretarial expenses	345	Sale of food	880
Cost of food	858	Dances	1,179
	5030		
Surplus of Income over Expenditure	1,072		
	6,102		6,102

*Balance Sheet of Waterfall Social Club
as at 31st May 19X3*

	£	£
Fixed Assets		
Hi-Fi equipment		1,220
Current Assets		
Cash in hand	830	
Less Current Liabilities		
Creditor for food	80	
Net current assets		750
Net assets		£1,970
Represented by:		
Accumulated fund:		
as at 1st June 19X2		898
Surplus for the year		1,072
		£1,970

Workings

1   Subscriptions

		£
Subs received		6,127
Less	Subs in arrear 1st June	278
		5,849
Add	Subs in arrear 31st May	220
		6,069
Add	Subs in advance 1st June	90
		6,159
Less	Subs in advance 31st May	135
	Subs for year	£6,024

2   Purchases of Regalia

		£
Purchases – Bank		1,145
Less	Owing 1st June	228
		917
Add	Owing 31st May	371
	PURCHASES =	1,288

3   Garage Tools

	£
Purchases – Bank	583
Add Net book value as at 31 May 19X8	1,550
	2,133
Value as at 31 May 19X9	1,450
DEPRECIATION =	£683

▶Task 1

Dr			SUBSCRIPTIONS A/c			Cr
19X8				*19X8*		
June 1	Balance (Subs in arrears) b/f	278		June 1	Balance (Subs in advance) b/f	90
19X9				*19X9*		
May 31	Subs in advance c/d	135		May 31	Bank	6,127
				"	Subs in arrears c/d	220
"	*Income & Expenditure	6,024				
		6,437				6,437
19X9				*19X9*		
June 1	Balance (Subs in arrears) b/d	220		June 1	Balance (Subs in advance) b/d	135

*See workings 1 for verification

▶Task 2

The Monarchs MCC Club
Regalia Trading A/c for the year ended 31st May 19X9

	£	£
Sales of Regalia		1,880
Less cost of sales		
Opening stock	255	
Add Purchases*	1,288	
	1,543	
Less Closing stock	298	1,245
PROFIT ON SALE OF REGALIA		£635

*See workings 2

123

▶Task 3

The Monarchs MCC Club
Income and Expenditure Account for the year ended 31st May 19X9

	£	£
Income		
Subscriptions*		6,024
Donations		350
Profit from sale of regalia		635
		7,009
Less expenditure		
Secretarial expenses	440	
Rent	2,750	
Meeting expenses	2,200	
Annual affiliation fee to National body	500	
Stationery and printing	345	
Depreciation*	683	6,918
EXCESS OF INCOME OVER EXPENDITURE		91

*See workings 1 and 3

Workings:

1   *Calculation of opening Accumulated Fund*

	£
Assets	
Equipment	3,480
Subscriptions in arrears	140
	3,620

Liabilities:	£	
Bank overdraft	950	
Subscriptions in advance	70	
Accrued expenses	260	
		1,280
Accumulated Fund		2,340

2   *Subscriptions account*

	£		£
Subscriptions in arrears b/f	140	Subscriptions in advance b/f	70
Subscriptions in advance c/d	100	Cash and Bank	6,220
Income and Expenditure	6,170	Subscriptions in arrears c/d	120
	6,410		6,410
Subscriptions in arrears b/d	120	Subscriptions in advance b/d	100

3 *Calculation of stationery and printing for the year:*

	£
Amounts paid	630
Less: Owing to suppliers b/f	260
	370
Add: Owing to suppliers c/f	350
	720

4 *Office Equipment*

	£	
Cost price	5,800	
Net book value 1st June 19X0	3,480	
Depreciation	2,320	– Year ended 31st May 19X0

		£	
Cost price	5,800		
Add: Additions	1,650	7,450	
Net book value 31st May 19X1		4,385	
Depreciation		3,065	– Year ended 31st May 19X1

∴ Current year's depreciation charge = £3,065 – 2,320 = £745

5   *Conference Account*

	£	£
Sale of Conference tickets		3,260
Less Conference expenses	770	
*Visiting speakers' expenses	1,680	2,450
SURPLUS ON CONFERENCE		810

* Visiting speakers' expenses

60% – Annual conference	60% of £2,800	= £1,680
40% – Conference expenses	40% of £2,800	= £1,120

▶Task 1

Academicals Society
Income and Expenditure Account for the year ended 31st May 19X1

	£	£
Income		
Subscriptions*		6,170
Surplus on conference		810
		6,980
Less Expenditure		
Secretarial expenses	1,450	
Rent	2,000	
Visiting speakers' expenses	1,120	
Donations to charity	570	
Stationery and printing	720	
Depreciation	745	6,605
EXCESS OF INCOME OVER EXPENDITURE		£375

▶Task 2

Academicals Society
Balance Sheet as at 31 May 19X1

	£
Fixed Assets:	
Equipment	
– at cost	7,450
– Less: depreciation	3,065
	4,385

	£	
Current Assets:		
Subscriptions in arrears	120	
Current Liabilities:		
Accrued expenses	350	
Subscriptions in advance	100	
Bank overdraft	1,340	
	1,790	

	£
Net Current Assets	(1,670)
Net Assets	2,715

	£
Represented by:	
Accumulated Fund:	
As at 1 June 19X0	2,340
Surplus for the year	375
	2,715

Workings

1 Subscriptions

	£
Received – year to 31 March 19X1	6,810
Received prior to 31 March 19X0	
(for year to 31 March 19X1)	420
	7,230
Received in arrear for year to	
31 March 19X0	252
SUBSCRIPTIONS	£7,482

2 *Trading Account re Sale of Photographic Equipment for the year ended 31 March 19X1*

	£	£
Sales		28,100
Less Cost of Sales		
Opening stock	3,420	
Add Purchases	22,734	
	26,154	
Less Closing stock	1,800	24,354
GROSS PROFIT		3,746

3 *Calculation of Profit/Loss on Disposal of Coach*

	£
Cost as at 1 April 19X0	18,000
Less Depreciation to date	
$\dfrac{£18,000}{5 \text{ years}}$ = £3,600 year × 4 years =	14,400
NET BOOK VALUE 31 MARCH 19X0	3,600
Less Proceeds of sale	2,560
LOSS ON DISPOSAL	£1,040

4 *Depreciation of Video Equipment*

	£
Cost 31 March 19X0	1,200
Less Depreciation	
$\dfrac{£1,200 - £200}{4 \text{ years}}$ = £250 year	250
	£950

5 *Accumulated Fund as at 31 March 19X0*

Assets	Cost	Depreciation	Net book value
Small transit coach	18,000	14,400	3,600
Video equipment (at cost)			1,200
Stock of photographic equipment			3,420
Balance at Bank			1,347
			9,567
Less Subscriptions in advance			420
ACCUMULATED FUND			9,147

▶**Task**

The High Towers Rural Pursuits Society
Income and expenditure account for the year ended 31 March 19X1

Income	£	£
Membership subscriptions: (See note 1)		
Year ended 31 March 19X0	252	
Year ended 31 March 19X1	7,230	
		7,482
Profit on sale of photographic equipment (Note 2)		3,746
Bank investment deposit account interest		82
		11,310
Less Expenditure		
Meeting room hire	340	
Stationery and postages	600	
Secretary's honorarium	300	
Printing year book	810	
National Society affiliation fee	180	
Depreciation – video equipment (Note 4)	250	
Loss on disposal of small transit coach (Note 3)	1,040	
Advertising for new members	230	
Lecturer for rural hobbies courses	460	4,210
Excess of income over expenditure		7,100

The High Towers Rural Pursuits Society
Balance Sheet as at 31 March 19X1

	£	£
Fixed assets:		
Land for proposed new meeting room and office, at cost		10,000
Video equipment: at cost	1,200	
Less: Provision for depreciation	250	950
		10,950
Current assets:		
Stock of photographic equipment	1,800	
Bank deposit account (£3,000 + £82)	3,082	
Balance at bank	745	
	5,627	
Less: Current liabilities		
Membership subscriptions received in advance	330	5,297
		16,247
Represented by:		
Accumulated fund at 1 April 19X0 (Note 5)	9,147	
Add: Excess of income over expenditure	7,100	16,247

Workings

1 *Calculation of Opening Capital – 1 September 19X7*

	Cost	Depreciation	Net Book Value
Assets	£	£	£
Motor vans A123 BWA	10,000	8,000	2,000
Stock			4,900
Debtors			7,320
Prepayments			160
Bank balance			1,970
			16,350
Less Liabilities			
Creditors		4,700	
Rent and rates owing		200	4,900
CAPITAL			£11,450

2

(a) *Purchases*	£	(b) *Sales*	£
Payments – Bank	72,000	Received – Bank	96,000
Discounts received	1,100	*Less:* Opening debtors	7,320
	73,100		88,680
Less: Opening creditors	4,700	*Add:* Closing debtors	9,500
	68,400	SALES	£98,180
Add: Closing creditors	2,590		
PURCHASES	70,990		

(c) *Rent and Rates* – Accrual	£	(d) *Insurance* – Prepayment	£
Paid – Bank	2,600	Paid – Bank	800
Less: In arrears 1.9.X7	200	*Add:* Prepaid 1.9.X7	160
	2,400		960
Add: In arrears 1.9.X8	260	*Less:* Prepaid 1.9.X8	200
RENT AND RATES	2,660	INSURANCE	760

3 *Motor Vehicles – Calculation of Profit or Loss on Disposal*

	£
Motor van A123 BWA Cost	10,000
Less: Depreciation to date	8,000
NET BOOK VALUE 1.9.X7	2,000
Proceeds from sales	2,100
PROFIT ON SALE	£100

4 *Depreciation of Motor Van*

	£
Motor Van E471 KBR Cost	13,000
Less: Depreciation (20% of £13,000)	2,600
NET BOOK VALUE 1.9.X8	£10,400

5   *Other Items to Note*

(a) – Bad debt £300 write off in Profit and Loss Account
     – Debtors £9,500 less bad debt £300 =   £9,200

(b) Introduction of extra capital
     Via sale of private yacht   £20,000

▶Task 1

Mary Grimes
Trading and Profit and Loss Account for the year ended 31 August 19X8

	£	£
Sales (Note 2 (b))		98,180
Less: Cost of sales – Opening stock	4,900	
Purchases (Note 2 (a))	70,990	
	75,890	
Less: Closing stock	5,900	
		69,990
Gross profit		28,190
Discount received		1,100
		29,290
Less: Rent and rates (Note 2 (c))	2,660	
Repairs and renewals	650	
Insurances (Note 2 (d))	760	
Wages	15,100	
Postages and stationery	1,360	
Motor vehicle expenses	3,350	
Motor vehicle depreciation	2,600	
Motor vehicle profit on sale (Note 3)	(100)	
Bad debt written off	300	
		26,680
Net profit		£2,610

▶Task 2

Mary Grimes
Balance sheet as at 31 August 19X8

	£ Cost	£ Depreciation	£ Net Book Value
Fixed assets			
Motor vehicle: At cost	13,000	2,600	10,400
Current assets			
Stock in trade	5,900		
Trade debtors (Note 5 (a))	9,200		
Amounts prepaid	200		
Balance at bank	2,010	17,310	
Less: Current liabilities			
Trade creditors	2,590		
Amounts accrued due	260	2,850	
Net Current Assets			14,460
			£24,860

Represented by:	£	£
Capital account: At 1.9.X7		
(Note 1)	11,450	
Add: Sale of private yacht	20,000	
Net profit	2,610	
	34,060	
Less: Drawings	9,200	
		£24,860

Workings

1
(a) Purchases

	£
Payment to suppliers	37,014
Less: Creditors 1.10.X8	2,150
	34,864
Add: Creditors 30.9.X9	786
PURCHASES	35,650

(b) Sales

	£
Received from debtors	60,205
Add: Takings not banked	5,500
	65,705
Less: Debtors 1.10.X8	358
	65,347
Add: Creditors 30.9.X9	241
SALES	65,588

(c) *Rent and Rates (Prepayment)*

	£
Paid via bank	7,500
Less: Paid in advance at 30.9.X9	824
RENT AND RATES	6,676

(d) *Electricity Charges (Accrual)*

	£
Paid via bank	1,201
Add: Owing at 30.9.X9	210
ELECTRICITY	1,411

2 *Depreciation*

Leasehold shop	£1,210
Shop equipment	£1,422

3 *Deposit Account*

	£
Balance 1.10.X8	6,412
Add: Transfer	500
	£6,912

4 *Drawings*

	£
Cash withheld	5,500
Via bank	1,047
	£6,547

▶Task 1

David's Fruiterer

Trading and Profit and Loss Account for the year ended 30 Sept 19X9

	£	£
Sales (Note 1 (b))		65,588
Less Cost of Sales		
Opening stock	931	
Add: Purchases (Note 1(a))	35,650	
	36,581	
Less: Closing stock	1,240	35,341
GROSS PROFIT		30,247
Less Expenses		
Rent and rates (Note 1 (c))	6,676	
Electricity (Note 1 (d))	1,411	
Wages	10,398	
Bank charges	314	
Sundry trade expenses	1,792	
Depreciation – Leasehold shop (Note 2)	1,210	
– Shop equipment (Note 2)	1,422	23,223
		7,024
Add: Interest from bank		428
NET PROFIT		£7,452

David's Fruiterer
Balance Sheet as at 30 Sept 19X9

	Cost £	Accumulated Depreciation £	Net Book Value £
Fixed Assets			
Leasehold shop	12,100	9,360	2,740
Shop equipment	19,634	13,007	6,627
	31,734	22,367	9,367
Current Assets			
Stock	1,240		
Debtors	241		
Prepayments	824		
Bank – Deposit A/c (Note 3)	6,912		
– Current A/c	835	10,052	
Less Current Liabilities			
Creditors	786		
Accruals	210	996	
NET CURRENT ASSETS			9,056
			£18,423
Financed by:			
Capital			17,518
Add: Net profit			7,452
			24,970
Less: Drawings (Note 4)			6,547
			£18,423

▶Task 1

Jane Simpson
Uncorrected Trial Balance as at 30 April 19X9

	£	£
Fixtures and fittings – at cost	8,000	
– provision for depreciation		3,000
Motor vehicles – at cost	9,600	
– provision for depreciation		5,600
Stock in trade	12,000	
Trade debtors	7,000	
Balance at bank	1,700	
Trade creditors		6,900
Sales		132,000
Cost of sales	79,200	
Establishment and administrative expenses	11,800	
Sales and distribution expenses	33,500	
Drawings	9,700	
Capital		30,000
	172,500	
Suspense account	5,000	
	£177,500	£177,500

▶Task 2

Jane Simpson
Trading and Profit and Loss Account for the year ended 30 April 19X9

	£	£
Sales		132,000
Less: Cost of sales – per trial balance	79,200	
Plus error in stock at 30 April 19X8	3,000	
	82,200	
Less: goods for own use	600	
		81,600
Gross profit		50,400
Less: Establishment and administrative expenses	11,800	
Sale and distribution expenses	33,500	
Depreciation – Fixtures and fittings	913*	
– Motor vehicles	2,400	
Sales commission	1,008	
		49,621
Net profit		£779

Jane Simpson
Balance Sheet as at 30 April 19X9

	£ Cost	£ Depreciation to date	£ NBV
Fixed assets:			
Fixtures and fittings	12,500	3,913	8,587
Motor vehicles	9,600	8,000	1,600
	22,100	11,913	10,187
Current assets:			
Stock	12,000		
Trade debtors (£7,000 + £500)	7,500		
Balance at bank	1,700		
		21,200	
Less: Current liabilities:			
Trade creditors	6,900		
Accruals – sales commission	1,008		
		7,908	
			13,292
			£23,479
Represented by: Capital account – At 1 May 19X8			30,000
Add: Adjustment to net profit year ended 30 April 19X8			3,000
			33,000
Add: Net profit year ended 30 April 19X9			779
			33,779
Less: Drawings (£9,700 + £600)			10,300
			£23,479

Workings

*Depreciation – Fixtures and fittings	£
10% of £8,000	800
10% of £4,500 for 3 months	113
	£913

▶Task 1

Work Sheet	Trial Balance		Adjustments		Trading A/c		Profit & Loss A/c		Balance Sheet	
	Dr	Cr	Dr	Cr	Dr	Cr	Dr	Cr	Dr	Cr
Capital		19,420								19,420
Equipment	3,750								3,750	
Furniture and fittings	2,000								2,000	
Motor vehicle	5,790								5,790	
Sales		32,010				32,010				
Purchases	19,740				19,740					
Bank	250								250	
General expenses	600						600			
Wages	5,940						5,940			
Rent, rates and insurance	2,550			200 (c)			2,350			
Heating and lighting	700		117 (b)				817			
Debtors	8,000								8,000	
Creditors		3,600								3,600
Stock 1.2.X2	5,710				5,710					
	55,030	55,030								
Stock 31.1.X3 (Asset)			4,910						4,910	
Stock 31.1.X3 ⎫										
Cost of goods sold ⎬				4,910 (a)		4,910				
Accrued expenses				117 (b)						117
Prepaid expenses			200 (c)						200	
			5,227	5,227						
Gross profit (balancing figure)					11,470			11,470		
					36,920	36,920				
Net profit (balancing figure)							1,763			1,763
							11,470	11,470	24,900	24,900

▶Task 2

S. Thorn
Trading and Profit and Loss Account for the year ended 31 January 19X3

	£	£
Sales		32,010
Less cost of sales		
Opening stock	5,710	
Add: Purchases	19,740	
	25,450	
Less: Closing stock	4,910	20,540
GROSS PROFIT		11,470
Less expenses		
General expenses	600	
Wages	5,940	
Rent, rates and insurance (£2550 – £200)	2,350	
Heating and lighting (£700 + £117)	817	9,707
NET PROFIT		£1,763

S. Thorn
Balance Sheet as at 31 January 19X3

	Cost	Depreciation	Net Book Value
Fixed assets	£	£	£
Furniture and fittings	2,000	–	2,000
Equipment	3,750	–	3,750
Motor vehicle	5,790	–	5,790
	11,540	–	11,540
Current assets			
Stock	4,910		
Debtors	8,000		
Prepayments	200		
Bank	250	13,360	
Less current liabilities			
Creditors	3,600		
Accruals	117	3,717	
Net current assets			9,643
			£21,183
Financed by			
Capital			19,420
Add net profit			1,763
			£21,183

▶Task 1

Work Sheet	Trial Balance		Adjustments		Trading A/c		Profit & Loss A/c		Balance Sheet	
	Dr	Cr	Dr	Cr	Dr	Cr	Dr	Cr	Dr	Cr
Purchases	73,936				73,936					
Sales		101,230				101,230				
Carriage inwards	245				245					
Carriage outwards	703						703			
Returns inwards and outwards	212	1,140			212	1,140				
Stock 1 Jan 19X9	4,910				4,910					
Wages and salaries	14,975						14,975			
Rent, rates and insurance	2,950		220	180			2,990			
Heating and lighting	627						627			
Motor vehicle	4,500			900					3,600	
Motor expenses	1,250						1,250			
Capital 1 Jan 19X9		18,948								18,948
Bank overdraft		2,819								2,819
Furniture and fittings	3,200								3,200	
Drawings	13,950								13,950	
Debtors	11,600								11,600	
Creditors		8,921								8,921
	133,058	133,058								
Stock 31 Dec 19X9 (Asset)			6021	(a)					6021	
Stock 31 Dec 19X9 Cost of goods sold				6021	(a)	6021				
Accruals – Rent				220	(b)					220
Prepayment – Rates			180	(c)					180	
Depreciation – Motor vehicle			900	(d)			900			
			7,321	7,321						
Gross profit (balancing figure)					29,088			29,088		
					108,391	108,391				
Net profit (balancing figure)							7,643			7,643
							29,088	29,088	38,551	38,551

▶Task 2

D. J. Lindhurst
Trading and Profit and Loss Account for the year ended 31 Dec 199X

	£	£
Sales		101,230
Less: Returns inwards		212
		101,018
Less Cost of goods sold		
Opening stock	4,910	
Add: Purchases	73,936	
Add: Carriage inwards	245	
	79,091	
Less: Returns outwards	(1,140)	
Less: Closing stock	(6,021)	71,930
GROSS PROFIT		29,088
Less Expenses		
Carriage outwards	703	
Wages and salaries	14,975	
Rent, rates and insurance	2,990	
Heating and lighting	627	
Motor expenses	1,250	
Depreciation – Motor vehicles	900	21,445
NET PROFIT		£7,643

D. J. Lindhurst
Balance Sheet as at 31 December 199X

	Cost	Depreciation	Net Book Value
	£	£	£
Fixed assets			
Furniture and fittings	3,200		3,200
Motor vehicle	4,500	900	3,600
	7,700	900	6,800
Current assets			
Stock	6,021		
Debtors	11,600		
Prepayments	180	17,801	
Less current liabilities			
Creditors	8,921		
Bank overdraft	2,819		
Accruals	220	11,960	
Net current assets			5,841
			£12,641
Financed by:			
Capital			18,948
Add: Net profit			7,643
			26,591
Less: Drawings			13,950
			£12,641

▶**Task**

Stamper
Trading and Profit and Loss Account for the year to 31 December 19X9

	£	£
Sales		150,750
Opening stock	25,600	
Purchases (112,800 − 450)	112,350	
Closing stock	−27,350	
Cost of goods sold		110,600
GROSS PROFIT		40,150
Wages	12,610	
Rent (2,500 − 500)	2,000	
Motor expenses (1,240 + 140)	1,380	
Depreciation:		
Motor vehicle (17,000 − 5,000)/4	3,000	
Equipment (15,000 − 4,500) × 30%	3,150	
Bad debt	200	
Insurance (1,000 + 450)	1,450	
		23,790
NET PROFIT		£16,360

Stamper
Balance Sheet as at 31 December 19X9

	£	£
Fixed assets		
Motor vehicle at cost	17,000	
Less Accumulated depreciation (3,000 + 3,000)	6,000	11,000
Equipment at cost	15,000	
Less Accumulated depreciation (4,500 + 3,150)	7,650	7,350
		18,350
Current assets		
Stock	27,350	
Debtors (9,950 − 200)	9,750	
Cash and bank (900 + 250)	1,150	
Prepayment	500	
	38,750	
Current liabilities		
Creditors	8,100	
Accrual	140	
	8,240	
Working capital		30,510
		£48,860
Financed by:		
Capital 1 January 19X9		52,500
Add Profit		16,360
		68,860
Less Drawings		20,000
		£48,860

▶Task

(a) *LIFO*

\multicolumn{9}{c}{STOCK LEDGER CARD – 3M GALVANISED GATES}

DATE	RECEIPTS			ISSUES			BALANCE	
	QTY	PRICE	£'s	QTY	PRICE	£'s	QTY	£'s
January	20	£30	600				20	600
March	4 / 20	£34	680				40	1,280
April				16	16 x £34	544	24	736
August	40	£40	1,600				64	2,336
December				48	40 x £40 4 x £34 4 x £30	1,600 136 120 1,856	16	480

(b) *FIFO*

\multicolumn{9}{c}{STOCK LEDGER CARD – 3M GALVANISED GATES}

DATE	RECEIPTS			ISSUES			BALANCE	
	QTY	PRICE	£'s	QTY	PRICE	£'s	QTY	£'s
January	4 / 20	£30	600				20	600
March	20	£34	680				40	1,280
April				16	£30	480	24	800
August	40	£40	1,600				64	2,400
December				48	4 x £30 20 x £34 24 x £40	120 680 960 1,760	16	640

(c) AVCO

STOCK LEDGER CARD – 3M GALVANISED GATES								
DATE	RECEIPTS			ISSUES			BALANCE	
	QTY	PRICE	£'s	QTY	PRICE	£'s	QTY	£'s
January	20	£30	600				20	600
March	20	£34	680				40	1,280
April				16	* £32	512	24	768
August	40	£40	1,600				64	2,368
December				48	** £37	17,76	16	592

Workings

```
*  20 × £30 =  600
   20 × £34 =  680
```

Av. price per gate $= \dfrac{(600 + 680)}{40} = £32$

```
** 24 × £32 =    768
   40 × £40 =  1,600
```

Av. price per gate $= \dfrac{(768 + 1,600)}{64} = £37$

►Task 1   (a) LIFO

STOCK LEDGER CARD

ITEM ___Metal Container___   CODE ___TQ 5450___

DATE	RECEIPTS			ISSUES			BALANCE	
19X3	QTY	PRICE	£'s	QTY	PRICE	£'s	QTY	£'s
Jan 1							1,000	7,500
Jan				750	£7.50	5,625	250	1,875
Feb	500	£10	£5,000				750	6,875
Mar				400	£10.00	4,000	350	2,875
April	750	£10.40	7,800				1,100	10,675
May	1,000	£10.80	10,800				2,100	21,475
June				1,100	1,000 x 10.80 10,800 100 x 10.40 1,040		1,000	9,635

(b) FIFO   STOCK LEDGER CARD

ITEM ___Metal Container___   CODE ___TQ 5450___

DATE	RECEIPTS			ISSUES			BALANCE	
19X3	QTY	PRICE	£'s	QTY	PRICE	£'s	QTY	£'s
Jan 1							1,000	7,500
Jan				750	£7.50	5,625	250	1,875
Feb	500	£10	5,000				750	6,875
Mar				400	250 x £7.50 1,875 150 x £10.00 1,500		350	3,500
April	750	£10.40	7,800				1,100	11,300
May	1,000	£10.80	10,800				2,100	22,100
June				1,100	350 x £10 3,500 750 x £10.40 7,800		1,000	10,800

▶Task 2

			Receipts			£
Feb	500	×	£10	=		5,000
April	750	×	£10.40	=		7,800
May	1,000	×	£10.80	=		10,800
						23,600

			Sales			£
Jan	750	×	£16	=		12,000
Mar	400	×	£16	=		6,400
June	1,100	×	£16	=		17,600
						36,000

Sandover & Sons
Trading Account for six months Jan–June

	LIFO		FIFO	
	£	£	£	£
Sales		36,000		36,000
Less cost of sales				
Opening stock	7,500		7,500	
Add: Purchases	23,600		23,600	
	31,100		31,100	
Less: Closing stock	9,635	21,465	10,800	20,300
GROSS PROFIT		£14,535		£15,700

▶Task 1

Calculation of Sales

				£
15 June	5,000	@	£30	150,000
30 June	5,000	@	£35	175,000
	10,000			325,000

Calculation of Purchases

8 June	7,000	@	£22	154,000
18 June	4,000	@	£24	96,000
22 June	2,000	@	£26	52,000
	13,000			302,000

▶Task 2

Units in Stock

Opening units	1,000
Purchased	13,000
	14,000
Sales	10,000
Closing stock units	4,000

► **Task 3**

Value of Closing Stock

FIFO basis	2,000	@	£24		48,000
	2,000	@	£26		52,000
					£100,000

LIFO basis	1,000	@	£20		20,000
	2,000	@	£22		44,000
	1,000	@	£24		24,000
					£88,000

Weighted Average Basis

Date			Units	Price £	Stock	Value £	Average £
June	1				1,000	20,000	20
	8	Purchased	7,000	22	8,000	174,000	21.75
	15	Sold	5,000	30	3,000	65,250	21.75
	18	Purchased	4,000	24	7,000	161,250	23.04
	22	Purchased	2,000	26	9,000	213,250	23.70
	30	Sold	5,000	35	4,000	94,778	23.70

► **Task 4**

Calculation of Gross Profit

	FIFO £	LIFO £	Weighted Average £
Opening Stock	20,000	20,000	20,000
Purchases	302,000	302,000	302,000
	322,000	322,000	322,000
Less closing stock	100,000	88,000	94,778
Cost of sales	222,000	234,000	227,222
Sales	325,000	325,000	325,000
Gross Profit	£103,000	£ 91,000	£ 97,778

The weighted average valuation gives a 'middle' value but this does not comprise *actual* value of any item in stock.

FIFO recovers costs in the order in which they were incurred, a logical basis, also, if LIFO is used and the issues do not exhaust the earlier stock quantities, then those items become a 'base' stock, valued at unrealistic prices if inflation continues.

▶Task 1

(a) FIFO   STOCK LEDGER CARD

ITEM _____ *Valve* _____   CODE __ *VX 4924* __

DATE	RECEIPTS			ISSUES			BALANCE	
	QTY	PRICE £	£'s	QTY	PRICE	£'s	QTY	£'s
April 1							180	3,240
3	360	17.70	6,372				540	9,612
9				240	180 x £18	3,240	300	5,310
					60 x £17.70	1,062		
15	120	18.15	2,178				420	7,488
20				240	£17.70	4,248	180	3,240
27	60	18.60	1,116				240	4,356
28				175	60 x £17.70	1,062	65	1,207
					115 x 18.15	2,087		
30	300	18.90	5,670				365	6,877

(b) LIFO   STOCK LEDGER CARD

ITEM _____ *Valve* _____   CODE __ *VX 4924* __

DATE	RECEIPTS			ISSUES			BALANCE	
	QTY	PRICE £	£'s	QTY	PRICE	£'s	QTY	£'s
April 1							180	3,240
3	120 ~~360~~	17.70	6,372				540	9,612
9				240	17.70	4,248	300	5,364
15	120	18.15	2,178				420	7,542
20				240	120 x £18.15	2,178	180	3,240
					120 x £17.70	2,124		
27	60	18.60	1,116				240	4,356
28				175	60 x £18.60	1,116	65	1,153
					115 x 18.15	2,087		
30	300	18.90	5,670				365	6,823

▶Task 1

(c) Cumulative Weighted Average Price

STOCK LEDGER CARD

ITEM _____ *Valve* _____   CODE _____ *VX 4924* _____

DATE	RECEIPTS			ISSUES			BALANCE	
	QTY	PRICE £	£'s	QTY	PRICE	£'s	QTY	£'s
April 1							180	3,240
3	360	17.70	6,372				540	9,612
9				240	£17.80	4,272	300	5,340
15	120	18.15	2,178				420	7,518
20				240	£17.90	4,296	180	3,222
27	60	18.60	1,116				240	4,338
28				175	£18.08	3,164	65	1,174
30	300	18.90	5,670				365	6,844

▶Task 2

(a) Periodic Weighted Average

Cost of Receipts for April: £

April	6	360	×	£17.70	=	6,372
	15	120	×	£18.15	=	2,178
	27	60	×	£18.60	=	1,116
	30	300	×	£18.90	=	5,670
		__840__				__15,336__

Number of units received in April   840 units

Cost per unit issued in April $\frac{£15,336}{840}$ = £18.257

           £

Value of opening stock (180 × £18)   3,240.00
Value of purchases in April   15,336.00
        18,576.00

Cost of Issues

April	9	240	×	£18,257	=	4,381.68	
	20	240	×	£18,257	=	4,381.68	
	28	175	×	£18,257	=	__3,194.97__	11,958.33

Value of stock   £ __6,617.67__

▶**Task 2**

(b) *Standard Cost*

Issue costs

						£
April	9	240	×	£18.00	=	4,320
	20	240	×	£18.00	=	4,320
	28	175	×	£18.00	=	3,150
						11,790

Closing stock at 30 April

			£
365	×	£18.00 =	6,570

	£
Value of materials plus closing stock	18,360
*Actual costs, plus opening stock	18,576
Difference	(216) ADVERSE

	£
*Receipts	£15,336
Opening stock	3,240
	£18,576

(c) *Replacement Cost*

Issue costs

						£
April	9	240	×	£18.15	=	4,356.00
	20	240	×	£18.50	=	4,440.00
	28	175	×	£18.50	=	3,237.50
						12,033.50

	£
Closing stock at April 30 365 × £18.90 =	6,898.50
Value of materials plus closing stock	18,932.00
Actual costs plus opening stock	18,576.00
Difference	£356.00

▶Task

	Skilled £	Unskilled £
Wages:		
50 hours × £6 × 52	15,600	
50 hours × £4 × 52		10,400
Lodging Allowance:		
48 weeks × £100	4,800	
48 weeks × £70		3,360
Food Allowance:		
48 weeks × £50	2,400	
48 weeks × £30		1,440
	£22,800	£15,200

Total Cost:

		£
4 skilled workers × £22,800	=	91,200
10 unskilled workers × £15,200	=	152,000
		£243,200

Total Hours

		Hours
48 weeks × 50 hours	=	2,400
Less: Idle time (5% of 2,400)	=	120
TOTAL HOURS WORKED PER EMPLOYEE		2,280

Total employees = 14 × 2,280 hours =   TOTAL HOURS WORKED   31,920

Group labour rate =

$$\frac{£243,200}{31,920 \text{ hours}} = £7.62 \text{ per hour per employee}$$

or Group £106.67

▶Task

Operation	Grade	Weekly Production	Worker Required	Weekly Rate Per Worker £	Weekly Cost £
Cutting	1	216	33	126.00	4,158.00
Sewing	2	108	67	138.60	9,286.20
Accessories	3	144	50	151.20	7,560.00
Pressing	4	270	27	126.00	3,402.00
Packaging	5	216	33	108.00	3,564.00
			210		27,970.20

Workings

1 *Weekly production* (per worker)

$$Cutting = \frac{36 \text{ hrs} \times 60 \text{ mins}}{10 \text{ mins}} = \frac{2,160}{10} = 216 \text{ units}$$

$$Sewing = \frac{36 \text{ hrs} \times 60 \text{ mins}}{20 \text{ mins}} = \frac{2,160}{20} = 108 \text{ units}$$

$$Accessories = \frac{36 \text{ hrs} \times 60 \text{ mins}}{15 \text{ mins}} = \frac{2,160}{15} = 144 \text{ units}$$

$$Pressing = \frac{36 \text{ hrs} \times 60 \text{ mins}}{8 \text{ mins}} = \frac{2,160}{8} = 270 \text{ units}$$

$$Packaging = \frac{36 \text{ hrs} \times 60 \text{ mins}}{10 \text{ mins}} = \frac{2,160}{10} = 216 \text{ units}$$

2 *Workers required*

$600 \times 12 = 7,200$ garments

$$Cutting \quad \frac{7,200}{216} = 33 \text{ workers}$$

$$Sewing \quad \frac{7,200}{108} = 67 \text{ workers}$$

$$Accessories \quad \frac{7,200}{144} = 50 \text{ workers}$$

$$Pressing \quad \frac{7,200}{270} = 27 \text{ workers}$$

$$Packaging \quad \frac{7,200}{216} = 33 \text{ workers}$$

3 *Weekly wages*

				£
Grade	1	36 hours × £3.50	=	126.00
	2	36 hours × £3.85	=	138.60
	3	36 hours × £4.20	=	151.20
	4	36 hours × £3.50	=	126.00
	5	36 hours × £3.00	=	108.00

▶**Task**

(a) (i) Premium should be regarded as overhead, charged to Factory Overhead Account and recovered over all production. However, if the premium is paid to fulfil a particular contract, it is likely to be included as a direct cost.

(ii) Incentive payment is normally related to output and should be regarded as a direct cost.

(iii) Sick and Holiday pay should be included in factory overhead rates.

(iv) Idle time is also an overhead, but it must be analysed and reported to management on a continuous basis.

(b) *Workings*

Calculate the Standard Performance Hours for each operator

Smith
$(15 \times 42) + (13 \times 60) + (11 \times 75) = 630 + 780 + 825 = \dfrac{2,235}{60}$ mins $= 37.25$ hours

Jones
$(15 \times 42) + (10 \times 60) + (8 \times 75) = 630 + 600 + 600 = \dfrac{1,830}{60}$ mins $= 30.50$ hours

Brown
$(15 \times 42) + (18 \times 60) + (16 \times 75) = 630 + 1,080 + 1,200 = \dfrac{2,910}{60}$ mins $= 48.50$ hours

Operator	Attendance	Standard Performance	Percentage Performance	Rate £	Gross Pay £
Smith	38	37¼	98	2.80	106.40
Jones	39	30½	78	2.40	93.60
Brown	42	48½	115	3.40	142.80

▶**Task**

(a) *If the current wage scheme is maintained:*

(i) *450 units*

450 × Time required of 40 mins	=	300 hours
Minimum guaranteed wage 10 × 36 hrs	=	360 hours
Total labour cost 360 hrs × £5	=	£1,800

(ii) *600 units*

600 × Time required of 40 mins	=	400 hours
Minimum guaranteed wage 10 × 36 hrs	=	360 hours
Total labour cost 360 hrs × £5	=	£1,800
plus overtime 40 hrs × £7.50	=	300
		£2,100

(iii) *750 units*

750 × Time required of 40 mins	=	500 hours
Minimum guaranteed wage 10 × 36 hrs	=	360 hours
Total labour cost 360 hrs × £5	=	£1,800
plus overtime 140 hrs × £7.50	=	£1,050
		£2,850

Ainsworth & Co.
Profit Statement (overheads ignored)

	Units		
	450	600	750
	£	£	£
Sales at £25 per unit	11,250	15,000	18,750
Less:			
Labour costs	(1,800)	(2,100)	(2,850)
Material costs at £10 per unit	(4,500)	(6,000)	(7,500)
PROFIT	4,950	6,900	8,400
PROFIT PER UNIT	£11	£11.50	£11.20

(b) *New scheme*

(i) *450 units*

450 × Time required of 35 mins	=	262.5 hours
Minimum guaranteed wage 10 × 36 hrs	=	360 hours
Total labour cost 360 hrs × £5.50	=	£1,980

(ii) *600 units*

600 × Time required of 35 mins	=	350 hours
Minimum guaranteed wage 10 × 36 hrs	=	360 hours
Total labour cost 360 hrs × £5.50	=	£1,980
plus overtime 10 hrs × £8.25	=	£ 82.50
		£2,062.50

(iii) *750 units*

750 × Time required of 35 minutes	=	437.5 hours
Minimum guaranteed wage 10 × 36 hours	=	360 hours
Total labour cost 360 hrs × £5.50	=	£1,980
plus overtime 77.5 hrs × £8.25	=	£ 639.37
		£2,619.37

Ainsworth & Co.
Profit Statement (overheads ignored)

	Units		
	450	600	750
	£	£	£
Sales × £25 per unit	11,250	15,000	18,750
Less:			
Labour costs	(1,980)	(2,063)	(2,619)
Material costs at £10 per unit	(4,500)	(6,000)	(7,500)
PROFIT	4,770	6,937	8,631
PROFIT PER UNIT	£10.60	£11.56	£11.51

(c) If the two schemes are compared the company makes more profit when lower production is achieved, i.e. £11.00 at output of 300 units under the existing scheme, compared to £10.60 under the new scheme. At higher volume of output an extra 31p profit is achieved.

The new scheme would only be worth introducing if the volume of output be constant at the higher volume of output (i.e. 750 units) or above, although the employees would be working to their maximum capacity if production was increased beyond 750 units.

SIMULATION 44ᴬ   Earnings Calculations

▶Task 1

(i) and (ii)

Output level		80 units	120 units	210 units
(a)	Piecework	£35.2	£36	£63
(b)	Premium bonus	£44	£44	£54.31

Workings of Piecework
Guaranteed wage = 80% (8 × £5.5)   £35.2
80 units Standard time 80 × 3 = 240 mins
∴ Piecework £24
120 units Standard time 120 × 3 = 360 mins
∴ Piecework £36
210 units Standard time 210 × 3 = 630 mins
∴ Piecework £63

Workings – Premium Bonus

Units	Time taken (mins)	Time allowed	Saved	Bonus
80	480	240	–	–
120	480	360	–	–
210	480	630	150	75% × 2½ hours × 5.5 = 10.31

Basic Pay 8 × £5.5 = £44

▶Task 2

Standard labour cost per unit = $\frac{5.5}{60} \times 3$ =		£0.275
Standard labour cost for period =	2,700 × £0.275 =	742.5
Actual cost		1,000.0
Total labour cost variance		(257.5) adverse

Labour rate variance		
Actual hours × standard rate	160 × £5.5 =	880
Actual hours × actual rate		1,000
		(120) adverse

Labour efficiency variance		
Standard hours × standard rate	135 × £5.5 =	742.5
Actual production hours × standard rate	140 × £5.5 =	770
		(27.5) adverse

Idle time variance		
Production hours worked	140 × £5.5 =	770
Actual hours paid	160 × £5.5 =	880
		(110) adverse

▶**Task**

Moores & Sons Ltd – Company Expenses

		Account
Rent of Factory		Factory O/h
Heating and lighting	– Factory	Ditto
	– Offices	Administration O/h
Insurance	– Plant and machinery	Factory O/h
	– Office equipment	Administration O/h
Advertising		Selling and Distribution O/h
Marketing manager's salary		Ditto
Printing and stationery	– Office	Administration O/h
	– Promotional material	Selling and Distribution O/h
Supervisor's wages	– Production	Factory O/h
Direct labour		Work in Progress O/h
Direct material		Ditto
Carriage outwards		Selling and Distribution O/h
Office salaries and wages		Administration O/h
Repairs and maintenance	– Plant and machinery	Factory O/h
	– Office equipment	Administration O/h
Direct expenses	– Royalties	Work in Progress O/h
Depreciation	– Plant and machinery	Factory O/h
	– Office equipment	Administration O/h
Salesman's commission and salary		Selling and Distribution O/h
New circular saw		Fixed Plant and Machinery

▶**Task**

Workings

Calculation of absorption rates

Depts	A	B	C
Works overheads	£15,000	£21,600	£28,800
Direct labour hours	6,000	8,000	9,000
Works overhead rate per direct labour hour	£2.50	£2.70	£3.20
Administration overhead	£8,610	£44,058	£26,934
Works cost	£61,500	£125,880	£269,340
Administration overhead as a percentage of works cost	14%	35%	10%

Cost Ledger Sheet Job No. ZS 23

Depts	A £	B £	C £	Total £
Direct material	1,950	2,820	690	5,460
Direct wages	2,400	900	1,995	5,295
Works overheads	1,250	1,080	1,920	4,250
WORKS COST	5,600	4,800	4,605	15,005
Administration overhead	784	1,680	461	2,925
TOTAL COST	6,384	6,480	5,066	17,930
Profit 30% of Total cost				5,379
SELLING PRICE				£23,309

▶**Task 1**

(i) *Absorption Rate* $\qquad \dfrac{\text{Budgeted Overhead}}{\text{Budgeted Direct Material Cost}} \times 100$

$= \dfrac{£200,000}{£100,000} \times 100$

$= \underline{200\%}$

(ii) *Absorption Rate* $\qquad \dfrac{\text{Budgeted Overhead}}{\text{Budgeted Machine Hours}} \times 100$

$\dfrac{£200,000}{£40,000} = \underline{£5}$ per machine hour

▶**Task 2**

Job D201

Materials used	£6,000
Overhead @ 200% =	£12,000

▶**Task 3**

Job D201

Machine hours worked	750
@ £5 per machine hour	£3,750

Overhead absorbed
  % on Direct Materials

			Overhead
Actual cost of materials		£140,000	Incurred
@ 200%	=	£280,000	£230,000
			Over absorbed £50,000

Machine hour rate

Actual machine hours		50,000	Incurred
@ £5 per machine hour		£250,000	£230,000
			Over absorbed £20,000

The over absorption should be transferred from the job cost account to an over/under absorption account, or if preferred, a separate *over* absorption account for subsequent transfer to costing profit and loss account as a profit. This balances out the excessive debit charged to profit and loss by the over absorption in the first place.

▶**Task 4**

(i) *Comparative job cost statements*

	Job D201 £		Job D201 £
Direct materials	6,000		6,000
Direct labour	3,000		3,000
Prime cost	9,000		9,000
Production overhead:			
200% on £6,000	12,000	M H R	
		750 × £5	3,750
Production cost	£21,000		£12,750

155

(ii) The merit of % on Direct Materials is that it is simple to calculate and apply and machine hours do not have to be recorded, but as illustrated above, it can have very misleading results. A job using expensive materials will be charged with much higher overhead cost than one using cheap materials even though the time taken to complete is the same for each job.

Consequently, if selling prices are fixed in relation to total costs the problem of overpricing and underpricing arises.

Overheads generally are a measure of lapse of time, e.g. indirect wages, rent, power, insurance, depreciation etc., so effect should be given to the time a job takes to complete. In the drilling department the overhead relates to machine use and the most accurate way would be to charge overheads to jobs on the basis of time spent on machines i.e. a machine hour rate.

SIMULATION 51ᴬ   Seddon's Manufacturers

▶Task 1

(a)   *Direct Labour Hour*
Calculation of hours used:

Forks 7,500 × 48 mins	=	6,000 hours
Spades 4,000 × 48 mins	=	3,200 hours
		9,200 hours

$$\frac{\text{Overhead}}{\text{Direct Labour Hours}} = \frac{£59,800}{9,200 \text{ hours}} = \underline{£6.50}$$

(b)   *Direct Materials Percentage Rate*

Forks 7,500 × £3.20	=	24,000
Spades 4,000 × £4.00	=	16,000
		£40,000

$$\frac{\text{Overhead}}{\text{Total Materials}} \times \frac{100}{1} = \frac{£59,800}{40,000} \times \frac{100}{1} = \underline{150\%}\text{ROUNDED}$$

(c)   *Direct Wages Percentage Rate*

Forks 7,500 × £2.40	=	18,000
Spades 4,000 × £4.00	=	16,000
		£34,000

$$\frac{\text{Overhead}}{\text{Total Wages}} \times \frac{100}{1} = \frac{£59,800}{34,000} \times \frac{100}{1} = \underline{175.8\%}$$

(d)   *Prime Cost Percentage Rate*

Forks 7,500 × £5.60	=	42,000
Spades 4,000 × £8.00	=	32,000
		74,000

$$\frac{\text{Overhead}}{\text{Prime Cost}} \times \frac{100}{1} = \frac{£59,800}{74,000} \times \frac{100}{1} = \underline{80.8\%}$$

▶Task 2

(a) *Direct Labour Hour*

	Fork £	Spade £
Prime Cost	5.60	8.00
Overhead:		
$\frac{£6.50}{60 \text{ mins}} \times 48\text{mins} =$	5.20	5.20
	£10.80	£13.20

(b) *Direct Material % Rate*

	Fork	Spade
Prime Cost	5.60	8.00
Overhead:		
150% of £3.20	4.80	
150% of £4.00		6.00
	£10.40	£14.00

(c) *Direct Wages % Rate*

	Fork	Spade
Price Cost	5.60	8.00
Overhead:		
176% of £2.40	4.22	
176% of £4.00		7.04
	£9.82	£15.04

(d) *Prime Cost % Rate*

	Fork	Spade
Prime Cost	5.60	8.00
Overhead:		
81% of £5.60	4.54	
81% of £8.00		6.48
	£10.14	£14.48

▶Task

1st Step – *Apportionment of Overheads to Departments*

Item	Basis of Apportionment	Total	A	B	C	Service
		£	£	£	£	£
Depreciation						
– Factory	Book value	2,800	560	672	952	616
– Equipment	Book value	1,575	315	378	536	346
Insurance						
– Equipment	Book value	525	105	126	179	115
Lighting	Floor area	875	206	206	309	154
Heating	Volume	700	166	177	238	119
Repairs and renewals						
– Factory	Floor area	875	206	206	309	154
Office costs	No. of employees	3,500	922	922	1,174	482
	TOTALS	10,850	2,480	2,687	3,697	1,986

2nd Step – *Allocation of Service Department Overheads to Manufacturing Departments* (35:40:25)

Manufacturing Department	Previous apportioned Overheads	Apportioned from Service Department	Total
	£	£	£
A	2,480	695	3,175
B	2,687	794	3,481
C	3,697	497	4,194
	£8,864 +	£1,986 =	£10,850

3rd Step – *Calculation of Total Unit Cost Using:*

(i)   *Unit Output Basis*

	Components		
	1	2	3
	£	£	£
Direct material (per unit)	16.00	19.00	30.00
Direct labour (per unit)	14.00	16.00	25.00
Absorbed overhead per unit (overhead ÷ output)	0.91	1.11	1.60
FULL COST	£30.91	£36.11	£56.60

(ii) *Machine Hour Basis*

	Components		
	1	*2*	*3*
	£	£	£
Direct material (per unit)	16.00	19.00	30.00
Direct labour (per unit)	14.00	16.00	25.00
Absorbed overhead per unit (overhead ÷ machine cost)	1.30	1.43	1.71
FULL COST	£31.30	£36.43	£56.71

Workings

Depreciation

Factory	=	£2,800			Equipment	=	£1,575		

							£
Book Value	=	£35,000	∴ Dept A	=	$\frac{35}{175} \times 2,800$	=	560
		42,000					
		59,500	B	=	$\frac{42}{175} \times 2,800$	=	672
		38,500					
		£175,000	C	=	$\frac{59.5}{175} \times 2,800$	=	952
			S	=	$\frac{38.5}{175} \times 2,800$	=	616
							£2,800

				£
∴ Dept A	$\frac{35}{175} \times 1,575$	=	315.00
B	$\frac{42}{175} \times 1,575$	=	378.00
C	$\frac{59.5}{175} \times 1,575$	=	535.50
S	$\frac{38.5}{175} \times 1,575$	=	346.50
			£1,575.00

Insurance

							£
Equipment	=	£525	∴ Dept A	$\frac{35}{175} \times 525$	=	105
Book Value			B	$\frac{42}{175} \times 525$	=	126
			C	$\frac{59.5}{175} \times 525$	=	178.5
			S	$\frac{38.5}{175} \times 525$	=	115.5
						£525

						£
Lighting	=	£875				
		Floor Area (Sq. metres)	$\therefore$			
Dept A		3,500	Dept A	$\dfrac{3,500}{14,875} \times 875$	=	206
B		3,500	B	$\dfrac{3,500}{14,875} \times 875$	=	206
C		5,250	C	$\dfrac{5,250}{14,875} \times 875$	=	309
S		2,625	S	$\dfrac{2,625}{14,875} \times 875$	=	154
		14,875 sq. metres				£875

						£
Heating	=	£700				
		Volume (cubic metres)	$\therefore$			
Dept A		11,025	Dept A	$\dfrac{11,025}{46,375} \times 700$	=	166
B		11,725	B	$\dfrac{11,725}{46,375} \times 700$	=	177
C		15,750	C	$\dfrac{15,750}{46,375} \times 700$	=	238
S		7,875	S	$\dfrac{7,875}{46,375} \times 700$	=	119
		46,375 cubic metres				£700

Repairs and Renewals
(Factory)   =   £875

Floor Area (Sq. metres)
(same as Lighting – see above)

						£
Office Costs	=	£3,500				
		(No. Employees)				
Dept A		88	Dept A	$\dfrac{88}{334} \times 3,500$	=	922
B		88	B	$\dfrac{88}{334} \times 3,500$	=	922
C		112	C	$\dfrac{112}{334} \times 3,500$	=	1,174
S		46	S	$\dfrac{46}{334} \times 3,500$	=	482
		334 employees				£3,500

▶Task 1

Departmental Overhead Distribution Summary
Budget Period (£'000s)

Expense	Allocation	Total	A	B	Stores	Maintenance	Tool Room
Indirect Labour	Direct	1,837	620	846	149	115	107
Supervision	No. of Employees	140	30	50	10	20	30
Power	Kw. Hours	160	80	40	4	20	16
Rent	Floor Area	280	50	125	55	30	20
Rates	Floor Area	112	20	50	22	12	8
Plant Insurance	Plant Value	40	20	16	–	2	2
Depreciation	Plant Value	20	10	8	–	1	1
		2,589	830	1,135	240	200	184
Stores	No. Requisitions		75	90	(240)	30	45
Maintenance	Hours		80	90	–	(230)	60
Tool Room	Hours		119	170			(289)
			1,104	1,485			
Machine Hours			55,200	99,000			
Absorption Rate per Machine Hour			£20	£15			

▶Task 2

Conversion cost is the sum of the production costs of converting purchased materials into finished products, i.e. direct wages, direct expenses and absorbed production overhead.

Added value is the increase in market value resulting from an alteration in the form, location or availability of a product or service, excluding the cost of bought-out materials and services.

The principal difference between the two terms is that Added Value includes profit whereas conversion cost does not.

▶Task 1

	Machinery	Finishing
Estimated overhead costs	£15,510	£6,400
Estimated production hours	2,350 M/C	1,280 DC Hrs
∴ Absorption rates	£6.60	£5.00

▶Task 2

	Machinery	Finishing	Maintenance
	£	£	£
Indirect material	2,900	1,600	1,750
Indirect labour	1,620	450	2,400
Depreciation	1,500	250	1,900
Lighting and heating	400	250	150
Supervision	1,420	710	980
Rent and rates	800	500	300
Insurances	1,200	200	1,600
	9,840	3,960	9,080
	6,474	2,606	(9,080)
	16,314	6,566	

▶Task 3

		Machinery	Finishing
Absorbed overhead	2,490 × £6.60	£16,434	
	1,320 × £5		£6,600
Actual		£16,314	£6,566
Over absorbed		£120	£34

▶Task 4

Expenditure	Budget	£15,510		£6,400	
	Actual	£16,314	(£804)	£6,566	(£166)
Volume	Budget Hours	2,350		1,280	
	Actual Hours	2,490		1,320	
		140 × £6.60 = £924		40 × £5 = £200	

▶Task 5

Allocation is more precise in that direct charging of specific overhead costs to cost centres or departments can be made with a degree of certainty. Effectively the overhead cost is a specific charge to the cost centre.

Apportionment is arbitrary – the cost is spread to departments on what is hopefully a fair and reasonable basis, e.g. rent and rates on the basis of area occupied, supervision costs based on the number of employees in each department.

▶Task 6

MACHINING DEPT					ASSEMBLY DEPT				
Actual cost	16,314	WIP	16,434		Actual cost	6,566	WIP	6,600
Over absorbed (P/L A/c)	120				Over absorbed (P/L A/c)	34		
	16,434		16,434			6,600		6,600

▶Task 1

Absorption Costing

	Small	Medium	Large	Total
	£	£	£	£
Marketing Personnel Salaries	15,000	9,000	3,000	27,000
Marketing Manager's Salary	12,000	2,000	6,000	20,000
Commission	1,000	1,200	800	3,000
Advertising	12,500	15,000	10,000	37,500
Packing and shipping	15,225	7,350	3,675	26,250
Delivery	11,020	5,320	2,660	19,000
Credit and collection	10,800	3,000	1,200	15,000
Marketing cost per order size	£77,545	42,870	27,335	147,750

Marketing cost as a percentage of total sales for each order size

% of Total Sales	Small	Medium	Large	Total
	$\frac{77,545}{250,000} \times 100$	$\frac{42,870}{300,000} \times 100$	$\frac{27,335}{200,000} \times 100$	$\frac{147,750}{750,000} \times 100$
	= 31%	14.3%	13.7%	19.7%

Workings

	Small	Medium	Large	Total
	£	£	£	£
1 Marketing Personnel Salaries				
No. of Personnel	5	3	1	9
$S = \frac{5}{9} \times 27,000 =$	15,000			
$M = \frac{3}{9} \times 27,000 =$		9,000		
$L = \frac{1}{9} \times 27,000 =$			3,000	27,000

	Small	Medium	Large	Total
	£	£	£	£
2 Marketing Manager's Salary				
Time Spent	60%	10%	30%	
$S = \dfrac{60}{100} \times 20{,}000 =$	12,000			
$M = \dfrac{10}{100} \times 20{,}000 =$		2,000		
$L = \dfrac{30}{100} \times 20{,}000 =$			6,000	20,000
3 Commission				
Amount of Sales	250K	300K	200K	750K
$S\ \dfrac{250}{750} \times 3{,}000 =$	1,000			
$M\ \dfrac{300}{750} \times 3{,}000 =$		1,200		
$L\ \dfrac{200}{750} \times 3{,}000 =$			800	3,000
4 Advertising				
Amount of Sales				
$S\ \dfrac{250}{750} \times 37{,}500 =$	12,500			
$M\ \dfrac{300}{750} \times 37{,}500 =$		15,000		
$L\ \dfrac{200}{750} \times 37{,}500 =$			10,000	37,500
5 Packing and Shipping				
Weight shipped				
$S\ \dfrac{6{,}090}{10{,}500} \times \dfrac{26{,}250}{1} =$	15,225			
$M\ \dfrac{2{,}940}{10{,}500} \times \dfrac{26{,}250}{1} =$		7,350		
$L\ \dfrac{1{,}470}{10{,}500} \times \dfrac{26{,}250}{1} =$			3,675	26,250

	Small	Medium	Large	Total
	£	£	£	£
6 Delivery Weight shipped				
S $\dfrac{6,090}{10,500} \times 19,000 =$	11,020			
M $\dfrac{2,940}{10,500} \times 19,000 =$		5,320		
L $\dfrac{1,470}{10,500} \times 19,000 =$			2,660	19,000
7 Credit and Collection No. of Orders				
S $\dfrac{612}{850} \times 15,000 =$	10,800			
M $\dfrac{170}{850} \times 15,000 =$		3,000		
L $\dfrac{68}{850} \times 15,000 =$			1,200	15,000

(b) *Marketing cost as a % of Total Sales*

S $\dfrac{77,545}{250,000} \times \dfrac{100}{1} = 31\%$

M $\dfrac{42,870}{300,000} \times \dfrac{100}{1} = 14.3\%$

L $\dfrac{27,335}{200,000} \times \dfrac{100}{1} = 13.7\%$

T $\dfrac{147,750}{750,000} \times \dfrac{100}{1} = 19.7\%$

▶**Task 2**

- Analysis in (1) above makes it clear that small orders are relatively more expensive to market.
- Medium and large orders are almost the same in terms of marketing costs to sales revenue:

  Medium 14.3%   Large 13.7%

- Large and medium orders are more cost effective:

	Small	Medium	Large	Total
Sales revenue	£250,000	£300,000	£200,000	£750,000
%	33%	40%	27%	100%
Marketing costs	£77,545	£42,870	£27,335	£147,750
%	52.5%	29%	18.5%	100%

- Large orders generate 27% of sales revenue and marketing costs are 18.5%, medium orders are similar but small orders are much less productive.

Basic information to be entered on Form VAT 100

Before you fill in this form **please read the notes on the back and the VAT Leaflet** *"Filling in your VAT return"*. Complete all boxes clearly in ink, writing 'none' where necessary. Don't put a dash or leave any box blank. If there are no pence write "00" in the pence column. Do not enter more than one amount in any box.

For official use		£	p
	VAT due in this period on **sales** and other outputs	1 26,250	00
	VAT reclaimed in this period on **purchases** and other inputs	2 11,025	00
	Net VAT to be paid to Customs or reclaimed by you **(Difference between boxes 1 and 2)**	3 15,225	00
	Total value of sales and all other outputs excluding any VAT. **Include your box 6 figure**	4 180,000	00
	Total value of **purchases** and all other inputs excluding any VAT. **Include your box 7 figure**	5 63,000	00
	Total value of all **sales** and related services to other **EC Member States**	6 30,000	00
	Total value of all **purchases** and related services from other **EC Member States**	7 3,000	00

Retail schemes. If you have used any of the schemes in the period covered by this return please enter the appropriate letter(s) in this box.   —

If you are enclosing a payment please tick this box.

DECLARATION by the signatory to be completed by or on behalf of the person named above.

I,..............*TOM AKHTAR*..............declare that the
(Full name of signatory in BLOCK LETTERS)

information given above is true and complete.

Signature.............................Date...*30th June*...19 *x3*

A false declaration can result in prosecution.

VAT 100   CD 2850/N9(02/91)   F 3790 (January 1992)

© Crown Copyright

Amount of VAT due:

		£
VAT on Outputs	=	26,250
VAT on Inputs	=	11,025
VAT PAYABLE		15,225

	£
Output Tax: Sales	3,109.81
Input Tax: Purchases	1,814.60
VAT PAYABLE	£1,295.21

Value Added Tax Return

For the period
to
1st Jan 19X2 to 31st March 19X2

Registration number

914 6159 66

Period

03x2

Mr. D. Bayley
Unit 30
West Park Industrial Estate
Bradford
Yorkshire

You could be liable to a financial penalty if your completed return and all the VAT payable are not received by the due date.

Due date: 30 04 x2

For official use D O R only

Before you fill in this form **please read the notes on the back and the VAT Leaflet** "*Filling in your VAT return*".
Complete all boxes clearly in ink, writing 'none' where necessary. Don't put a dash or leave any box blank. If there are no pence write "00" in the pence column. Do not enter more than one amount in any box.

For official use		£	p
VAT due in this period on **sales** and other outputs	1	3,109	81
VAT reclaimed in this period on **purchases** and other inputs	2	1,814	60
Net VAT to be paid to Customs or reclaimed by you **(Difference between boxes 1 and 2)**	3	1,295	21
Total value of **sales** and all other outputs excluding any VAT. **Include your box 6 figure**	4	17,730	00
Total value of **purchases** and all other inputs excluding any VAT. **Include your box 7 figure**	5	10,369	00
Total value of all **sales** and related services to other **EC Member States**	6	NIL	00
Total value of all **purchases** and related services from other **EC Member States**	7	NIL	00

Retail schemes. If you have used any of the schemes in the period covered by this return please enter the appropriate letter(s) in this box.   —

If you are enclosing a payment please tick this box.

DECLARATION by the signatory to be completed by or on behalf of the person named above.

I,......DENNIS BAYLEY..declare that the
(Full name of signatory in BLOCK LETTERS)

information given above is true and complete.

Signature ....Date 31st March 19 x2

A false declaration can result in prosecution.

VAT 100   CD 2850/N9(02/91)   F 3790 (January 1992)

Output Tax	£	£	£
17½% of £110,800			19,390
Input Tax			
Re: Taxable supplies		11,080	
Re: Overheads (80% of 2,920)		2,336	
Re: Exempt supplies	1,083		
plus Overheads (20% of 2,920)	584	1,667	15,083
VAT PAYABLE			£ 4,307